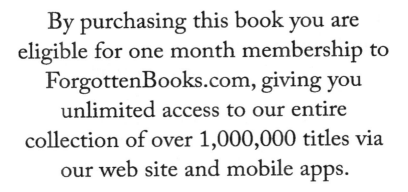

English
Français
Deutsche
Italiano
Español
Português

www.forgottenbooks.com

Mythology Photography **Fiction**
Fishing Christianity **Art** Cooking
Essays Buddhism Freemasonry
Medicine **Biology** Music **Ancient
Egypt** Evolution Carpentry Physics
Dance Geology **Mathematics** Fitness
Shakespeare **Folklore** Yoga Marketing
Confidence Immortality Biographies
Poetry **Psychology** Witchcraft
Electronics Chemistry History **Law**
Accounting **Philosophy** Anthropology
Alchemy Drama Quantum Mechanics
Atheism Sexual Health **Ancient History**
Entrepreneurship Languages Sport
Paleontology Needlework Islam
Metaphysics Investment Archaeology
Parenting Statistics Criminology
Motivational

INVESTOR

BY

EDWARD SHERWOOD MEAD, Ph.D.

PROFESSOR OF FINANCE IN THE WHARTON SCHOOL OF FINANCE
AND COMMERCE, UNIVERSITY OF PENNSYLVANIA

PHILADELPHIA & LONDON
LIPPINCOTT COMPANY

Printed by J. B. Lippincott Company
At the Washington Square Press
Philadelphia, U. S. A.

ISBN 978-1-330-05085-9
PIBN 10013455

PREFACE

AMERICAN investors, under our crude and careless methods of finance, have lost incalculable amounts of money by purchasing bad securities. Not alone has the "get-rich-quick" company preyed upon the investor, but hundreds of millions have been lost in the bonds and stocks of railroad, public-service, and industrial corporations—securities often issued under the auspices of responsible and respected banking houses, but which, either because of defects in the securities which a careful preliminary examination would have disclosed, or because of bad financial management, have failed to come up to expectation.

Made wise by costly experience, the American investor has grown critical in recent years. He is disinclined to speculate. He looks for security before income. He asks many questions concerning assets, earnings, the quality of management, the strength of franchises, the extent of monopoly control possessed by the companies into which he puts his money. It is no longer easy to victimize him with junior lien mortgage bonds or with inflated stocks.

Investment bankers have also learned that a reputation for sound judgment as to the value of the securities which they offer is their greatest asset. Competition for the investors' money is growing constantly more strenuous. Salesmen are quick to seize upon the weak points in the securities offered by other houses. The banker cannot afford to take chances by selling bonds of whose merits he has not thoroughly satisfied himself.

Out of the growing caution of the investor in buying securities, and the desire of the investment banker to take no chances as to the quality of what he offers, has been developed a body of sound financial knowledge which is constantly being utilized to increase the security of investments. Improvement has proceeded so far that it is now possible to offer the investor thoroughly safe bonds which will yield a much higher rate of interest than was, until recent years, thought consistent with security.

This book, the outgrowth of a series of magazine articles which has followed a fairly consistent plan of arrangement, aims to present some of the

PREFACE

accepted opinions as to what constitutes a safe investment. The·author claims no special ability in indicating sound investments, but he is confident that close adherence to the cautions laid down in the following pages will keep the investor from buying investments which are unsound.

EDWARD SHERWOOD MEAD

PHILADELPHIA, 1914

CONTENTS

9

THE
CAREFUL INVESTOR

I

THE CHANCES OF A LAMB IN THE STOCK MARKET

COMPLAINTS of the extreme dulness in business are rife in all stock brokerage houses. The "public" is not buying stocks. Brokers are reduced to the expedient of preying upon one another. Meantime expenses continue, and there is no relief in sight. "For this condition," said a veteran broker, "the muck-raking magazines are responsible. They have denounced Wall Street and Wall Street methods so persistently and with such violence that the people have come to look on the term 'Banker and Broker' with suspicion. They do not want to trust brokers with their money. They feel that they will not be treated fairly. They do not believe that the Wall Street game is honest."

11

"Is it honest?" he was asked. "Are the people correct in their opinions? What about this criticism of the financial game? Do you believe there is anything in it?"

"Well," he replied, "I'll tell you my own opinion. The magazines are right. There's nothing in the game for the people except excitement, worry, and loss. If a man sticks to the stock-market game long enough, he will lose. While he is playing it, unless he is careful, he will be made the victim of some trick of manipulation which will take his money away from him, without even giving him a run for it. Of course, it's my living. I like the business. I try to be fair to my customers; I know I am honest with them; but sometimes, when I stop to think, I'm sorry for them. They haven't a chance."

Such candor is unusual and refreshing. Read the solemn editorials in the newspapers when it is proposed to abolish or restrict the stock exchange. Note the indignation with which any such proposals are received. "Without the stock exchanges and the brokers," we are assured, "business could not be carried on." It is admitted that there are abuses. Foolish men speculate to their ruin. Occasionally a broker turns rogue, makes a dishonest failure because he speculated for his own account with the money of his customers. But these are only incidents. They furnish no reason, it is said, to overthrow a great and beneficent institution, or even to hamper or seriously interfere with its operations. Through the stock exchanges capital is mobilized, brought together in great masses for railroads and subways. The buying and selling of the brokers for their customers and for themselves establishes the values of stock and bonds. The stock exchange discounts future events. If the corn crop is threatened by drought, down go the prices of Western railroad stocks. Is a trust threatened with attack? The stock exchange knows before any one else, and the ticker tells the story. Without the stock exchange, the banks could not make loans on collateral with any safety, since they would have difficulty in finding a quick market in case it became necessary to sell.

These are strong statements. They have high authority to support them. They are not to be questioned without the production of strong evidence that they are overdrawn. Certainly, they will not be questioned here.

While, however, we may recognize the stock

exchange and the members thereof as public bene-
factors, indispensable parts of the intricate plan
of things as they are, it is well to look at the situation of the man or the woman who makes the
stock exchange and the brokers possible—the
margin speculator. It is the speculator who pays
the commissions. The commissions build the exchanges, pay the rents of the brokers' offices,
maintain the costly private wires, and support the
modest establishments of the thousands of men
who get their living from the business. The bills
for these are heavy. The speculator pays these
bills. What does he get for his money?

First, let us clearly understand the nature of
margin speculation as carried on through a stock
exchange house. You, let us say, are a merchant.
You have a good bank balance or some sound
investments. You believe that Atchison common at par is too low. You think the price will
advance. You resolve to take advantage of the
rise. You secure an introduction to a broker.
How glad he is to see you—especially in times
like these. You give him an order to buy 500
shares of Atchison, costing $50,000, for your
account and risk.

You do not have $50,000. Your available resources are only $5,000. But this is no barrier to the transaction. Your broker is also a banker. He will lend you the difference between $5,000 and $50,000, and will buy the 500 shares for you, providing you will leave the stock on deposit with him to secure the loan. The purchase is made. You give the broker $5,000 in cash or securities. He borrows $45,000 from a bank or trust company and buys 500 shares of Atchison, as he notifies you, "for your account and risk."

I once heard a broker describe the resulting situation and its developments as follows.

Says the broker to his customer, or "client": "You own 500 shares of Atchison, costing $50,000, and worth $50,000 to-day. Of this $50,000, $5,000 is your money and $45,000 is my money. Suppose, now, that the price of Atchison goes up 10 points. Your 500 shares are worth $55,000. Of this $55,000, $10,000 is your money and $45,000 is my money. You have made $5000. Suppose, now, that you have had enough for the present. You have vindicated your judgment of Atchison's value. You have a good opinion of yourself. You decide to rest on your oars and take your profits. You order your broker to sell. Your account with your broker stands like this.

John Jones in account with Smith & Company, Bankers and Brokers.

Dr.		Cr.	
To loan..............	$45,000	By 500 shares A.T.S.F.	$55,000
To interest 1 month 6 per cent..........	225		
To commission ¼ per cent..............	125		
	$45,350		
Balance..........	9,650		
	$55,000		$55,000

The broker now gives you, if you want it, a check for $9,650—your original $5,000, and $4,650 additional. You are a successful speculator. Life is sweet.

Now reverse the situation. Atchison does not go up. It goes down. The grasshopper, or the hot winds, or the Kansas legislature, or the Interstate Commerce Commission, move on the Atchison. Atchison common is "weak." It goes down two points. Comes now your broker and says to you, in effect, something like this: "You own 500 shares of Atchison. These shares are worth today $49,000. Of this $49,000, $45,000 is my money and $4,000 is your money." Suppose the hot wind blows on, and Atchison goes down three points more. Again your broker confronts you.

"Your 500 shares are worth only $47,500. Of this sum $45,000 is my money and $2,500 is your money. I have these shares pledged at the bank as collateral for the $45,000 I borrowed for you. The bank demands more security. I'm sorry, but I must have more margin. About $1,000 will be sufficient." So you give the broker $1,000 more, and if Atchison keeps on descending, you give him another $1,000, and another. You must keep his security safe. He must always have $45,000 in the value of your stock.

Now, suppose you cannot meet these calls for margin. Suppose Atchison goes down 10 points in a single day—it went down 18 points on May 18, 1901—and you cannot raise the money for margins. You are sold out. Your broker sells your 500 shares of Atchison, if he is honest, at the best price he can get; if he is dishonest, at the lowest price of the day. He sends you this statement:

John Jones in account with Smith & Company, Bankers and Brokers.

Dr.		Cr.	
To loan..............	$45,000	By 500 shares A.T.S.F.	
To interest..........	225	@ 92	$46,000
To commission.......	125		
Balance due Jones....	650		
	———		———
	$46,000		$46,000

THE CAREFUL INVESTOR

You have lost $4,350, perhaps in a single day. This is margin speculation. This is what keeps the stock exchanges and the brokers' offices going.

There are two questions to ask about speculation. First, is this the best way to speculate? and, second, what is the chance of profit in speculation? A few years ago, in a large Eastern city, there was a stock exchange house that was supposed to be impregnable. The partners were popular and respected. They were closely related to two of the wealthiest families in the city. The firm was reported to have ample capital. One morning this firm closed its doors. Its liabilities were enormous. Most of its assets had disappeared. No explanations were forthcoming. The creditors were called together and informed that, for family reasons, relatives of the firm would make up most of the shortage, provided there was no prosecution. Another house in the same city recently failed. It paid to unsecured creditors ten cents on the dollar.

Cases like these usually involve breaches of trust between broker and client. You give the broker your money to secure him in borrowing a much larger amount of money with which to buy 500 shares of Atchison stock for you. You leave the stock with him as security for your loan. It is your stock. The law says that your broker must hold it for you. He can pledge it at the bank, but he must pledge it' for your benefit, so that whenever you want to pay the balance due, you can have the stock. If your broker pledges this stock for his own benefit, or in any way puts it out of his power to deliver you these 500 shares when you come for them, the law of New York and Pennsylvania says he is guilty of larceny. If your broker obeys the law and keeps your securities for you, he might, indeed, fail in business. His own funds might be eaten up in speculation for his own account, or in expenses, but his failure would disclose no "unsecured creditors." No one would lose except himself.

When you deal with a broker on this basis of depositing margin, you depend absolutely upon his good faith and fear of the law. If he chooses to use for his own benefit the stocks which belong to you, you cannot stop him, for, as long as he remains solvent, you will know nothing about the matter. There is no inspection of brokerage houses. They are all partnerships. There is no bank examiner to go over the books. The customers of brokerage houses are absolutely at their mercy.

If a safe method of margin speculation could be

suggested, surely no one would deal through the broker. Yet such a method is available to any one with a substantial bank account. If you have faith in the Atchison; if you believe it is going up; if you are not content with the profits on 50 shares which you have the money to buy and pay for; if you want the profits on a large number of shares,—go to your banker. Give him your order. He will lend you 80 per cent on any Atchison stock which you may own, and he will buy the stock for you through some broker, charging you only the broker's commission. You cannot buy as many shares through your banker as through a broker, but in all other respects the transaction to you is the same as though you had dealt through the "banker and broker."

The bank buys the stock for you. You pay the bank $5,000. You sign a note for the balance of the purchase price. It is your stock. The certificate is made out in your name. Your note is pinned to the certificate, and it goes along with it. The bank does not use your stock for its own purposes, for the bank is a public institution, a corporation with a regular organization. Whatever it does must be known to the officers or directors. Its accounts are published. It is subject to the inspection of the bank examiners. You know that when you buy stock on margin through your bank you may lose your money, but your loss will be the result of your own bad judgment, and not of the larceny of a broker.

Since, now, as speculators in stocks on margin, we have found a safe way to speculate, what are our chances of profit? They are poor, very poor, almost negligible. Space does not permit at this time any extended discussion of the reasons why the margin speculator has no chance. Let two cases suffice where speculation on the most positive information went wrong.

Many years ago, an Eastern railroad was in trouble. It was a large producer of coal, which it sold through agents. One firm of agents had positive information, which came to them in the course of business, that bankruptcy was inevitable. They knew it, and subsequent events proved that they were right. They resolved to take advantage of this knowledge in the stock market. They raised $30,000, all the money they could get together, and they sold this stock short on a 10 point margin. That is to say, they made a contract through their brokers with certain other brokers to lend them 15,000 shares of this stock, and they agreed to deliver 15,000 shares on demand. This stock they sold for $300,000, leaving the $300,-000, together with the original $30,000, with the broker to secure the transaction. They expected that the stock would drop to 10. Then they would order the broker to buy 15,000 shares, which would cost only $150,000; return the shares to the brokers from whom they had borrowed them, and receive from the brokers the difference between $300,000 and $150,000, less the brokers' charges as their profit. They would also get back their original stake of $30,000.

Now, observe. The information was accurate. The railroad company was in a bad way. It did fail—later. Its stock did drop, not only to 10 but to 5—later. At the time, however, certain powerful and wealthy men decided to put the price of this stock up, and by heavy buying they did put it up to 25. Our friends the coal dealers were caught in the rise. Their broker was asked to return the 15,000 shares. He bought these shares at 22, costing $330,000. The $30,000 was gone. The firm failed, and it was no comfort to them that the railroad failed soon after.

One more instance. A prominent attorney was employed by certain stockholders to bring suit **to** dissolve a large company whose stock was active on the exchange. The announcement of the suit was sure, as he thought, to break the price of the stock. So he raised $15,000 and sold the stock short. Now, mark, his information was accurate. He himself had drawn the papers. He himself was to file them. He was to give out the news. The news would break the price of the stock at least 10 points. He was certain to double his money. The stock was sold at ten o'clock, immediately after the opening of the exchange. At noon, announcement was made that this company would be merged with others into a large company. The suit was withdrawn. Immediately the stock advanced. The lawyer was fortunate to escape with the loss of half his stake.

Here are two cases where shrewd and intelligent men, "on the inside," possessed of accurate and exclusive information, tried to turn their knowledge into money and failed. Such cases are not exceptional. The wisest speculator this country ever produced said that he was satisfied to be right four times out of seven. The speculator of average intelligence and good fortune can be sure of one thing: that if he sticks long enough at the game, he will lose all he puts in.

THE CAREFUL INVESTOR

I do not wish to be understood as saying that it is not possible to buy stocks in part with borrowed money when prices are low, and profit by the advance. This is possible, and is not attended with serious risks if the purchaser is careful to maintain large margins for his loans; if he buys dividend-paying stocks, the income on which will offset the interest on his loans; and if he is satisfied to wait. I do not believe that there is much risk in the purchase of sound railroad stocks on this basis. Eventually—it may be after the lapse of years, but some day—the purchase will probably show a profit. But for the margin speculator, for the trader who buys and sells on tips and rumors, who is in and out of this or that stock, against whom 6 per cent. interest is always running, and who must pay $25 commission on every block of 100 shares, for the great army of the "public," the people who pay the brokers' bills, who keep the Stock Exchanges running, there is a certainty of just one thing: certain and total loss.

A broker once told me that there was one rule which he would give, if he dared, to his customers, to guide them in selecting stocks for trading purposes. "Take a piece of chewing gum. Reduce it to an adhesive condition. Mould it into a form convenient for throwing. Throw it at the quotation board. Buy or sell, according to the toss of a coin, the stock indicated by the spot on the board to which the chewing gum adheres. Go to Europe for three months." By following this advice, he said, the customer would have a chance —not much of a chance, it is true, but some chance. If, however, he reads the financial page of the newspaper, and listens to the gossip in the brokers' offices, he has not even the gambler's chance, since he will be doing exactly what the powers back of the market want him to do, that they may as quickly as possible get his principal before it is exhausted by the constant nibbling of the broker.

A well-to-do man showed his *ingénue* bride a check for $1,800. "Do you see this check? Now, with this I'm going to buy sugar. Sugar is going up, and I'll give you the profits." Sugar went down, and he lost his $1,800. The lady asked for an accounting. "My dear, sugar went down. The money is lost." "And you haven't any sugar," she asked plaintively, "not even any sugar?"

It will be well for the American people if the present dullness in brokerage circles, in so far as this dullness represents increasing knowledge of the pitfalls of margin speculation, shall continue. For money making, margin speculation is worthless. As a means to loss and ruin, it has no rivals.

So much for the traders. What now of the brokers? Do they make money, and how much do they make?

A stock brokerage business is profitable under ordinary conditions *if the broker does not trade for his own account.* On a certain mildly active day on the Philadelphia Exchange—a very small affair compared with the New York Exchange—a broker told me that his commissions amounted to $750 on that day's business, and his business is not of the first rank, even for Philadelphia. If only the broker will keep out of the market for his own account, and confine himself to working for his "clients," he is pretty sure to succeed.

Providing the necessary police arrangements can be made, all branches of the gambling business, from stuss to faro, are extraordinarily profitable. Even if the games are honestly conducted, providing only that the house has ample capital, the returns are more certain than in any other branch of pecuniary activity. But when the keeper of the gambling house turns gambler, the testimony is unanimous that he is sure to lose.

A LAMB IN THE STOCK MARKET

So in the stock market game, in which more gambling is done than in all other games of chance combined, the people who make money are those who keep the game, who take their percentage in commissions and interest on every transaction. The players in this game, as in every other game of chance, are sure to lose. Surely if the men who live in daily contact with the security market cannot make money out of operations in stocks, the outsider has even less chance of profit.

But what of the study of "fundamental conditions"? If we study crops, earnings, interest rates, etc., can we not make money in stock speculation? Is it not a fact that brokers are too close to the market to take proper account of its underlying tendencies? Is not the stock market far different from the roulette table? Can we not predict from a study, say, of Reading or United States Steel, the future course of these stocks, and make money by following our conclusions with our money?

Some years ago a wealthy New York merchant retired from business. His fortune ran into seven figures. He was well educated, well informed, studious. He enjoyed a wide acquaintance among bankers and business men. He himself was a director in several banks, and in a position to hear the latest and most accurate information affecting security values. He decided, for the remainder of his active life, to occupy his mind in operations in stocks. He applied to this business the same care and attention that had brought him his fortune. He was very conservative. He bought only after a careful study of underlying business conditions, as well as of the circumstances of the particular companies in which he was interested. He had ample capital to follow his operations to a conclusion. For seven years he dealt in stocks. In that time his purchases and sales totaled over $12,000,000, and showed a profit of less than $1,000 as the reward for large capital and a first-class business man in stock speculation.

My belief, based on a somewhat extended observation of the work which students of fundamental conditions are doing, is that what I have described as the "chewing gum" method of speculation is, in the long run, about as safe as speculation based on a study of "underlying conditions."

Especially is the studious speculator urged to do his own studying and to avoid the professional stock-market educators. Every one knows who they are. I am acquainted with several of them who are doing very well indeed in selling predictions based on "a study of fundamental conditions" to persons who are willing to pay a good price each month for the "service." For thirty dollars a month, you can have daily converse with one of these schoolmasters who will tell you when and what to buy and sell. It makes little difference in the final result. You will perhaps lose your money in less time, and the broker will get less of it by the amount you pay for education. Some of these students have lost a great deal of money by taking the advice which they sold to others.

I do not believe that any man, or any committee or congregation of men, no matter how well informed, can safely advise the purchase or sale on margin of speculative securities. Accurate predictions in this field are very difficult. Prices are "made," to a large extent, on the stock exchanges. Ask your broker, if you can find him in a confidential mood, whether he ever "matches" orders. Of course he does. When a pool is formed to raise the price of a stock, orders are distributed both to buy and to sell. The members are dealing, through brokers, with one another. They mark up the quotations, hoping to attract a public following, who will take the stocks they have accumulated off their hands at a profit. Sometimes the instructions are misunderstood, and the game is given away by a jump of thirty points in Rock Island in half an hour. In that case, the broker who had the selling order was snowbound, or sick, or otherwise unavailable, and when the buying order was executed, there was no stock for sale. The Stock Exchange severely disciplined the offenders.

While the pool is working, the newspaper men are fed with news calculated to help along the movement. Rumors that "Frick is buying into the company," or that "the Erie will purchase the road," or that "a conflict for control of the company is in progress," are passed out, and sometimes printed, although it is not so easy as it once was to fool the financial editor. If the public is attracted and buys the stocks, the pool may change to the bear side and sell short. Then another set of rumors is set afloat. "There is friction in the Union Pacific Board," "The Harriman estate is selling out its stock," etc., etc. The president of a large Western railroad recently said that the only trouble with the stock of his company was the "lie factory in Wall Street."

I do not wish to be misunderstood. Stocks do rise and fall from certain fundamental causes. A crop failure, for example, ought to produce a decline in the stocks of railroads located in the region affected. But suppose that the crop failure comes during a boom year, when business all over the country is expanding; or that a failure in the wheat and corn traffic is offset by a rapid growth in oil and coal; or that the company has been very conservative in the management of its income, has paid out in dividends only half its earnings, and now makes a special distribution to its stock-holders. In such case, crop failure might be more than neutralized by the favorable influences, and the "scientific" speculator who had sold "short" because, after a careful study of rain-fall statistics, he had reached the correct conclusion that there would be a short crop in the south-west and a reduction in railroad earnings, might lose his entire stake, in spite of correct reasoning.

Is there no safe method of speculating on margin? Cannot a man with $5,000, for example, employ this to control $50,000 of stock, so that if the price of this stock advances ten points, he can double his money? I know of two methods which are relatively free from danger, and since I have said so much against margin speculation, these methods ought to be explained.

In recent years many railroads and a few industrial corporations have been issuing a security known as a "convertible debenture." A debenture bond is a promise of a corporation to pay the bearer or registered owner $1,000 in, say, 1943. Suppose the company has $5,000,000 of these debentures outstanding, on which it pays five per cent. interest, or $250,000 a year. The company's profits available for interest payments may be $1,000,000 a year. In such a case the debentures would be good. They would usually sell between 90 and 100 per cent. of the par value, sometimes rising to 100 and sometimes falling to 90.

Now, suppose that this company, needing additional funds, decides to issue $10,000,000 of debentures in place of this $5,000,000, providing $5,000,000 of cash and retiring the old issue by exchange. In order to make the new bonds attractive, they are made convertible into stock at par. That is to say, any holder of a $1,000 debenture bond can at any time exchange it for ten shares of stock.

Now observe what happens. If the company prospers, and raises the rate of dividend on its stock from 6 per cent. to 12 per cent., the stock may advance from, say, 90 to 175. Since the debenture bonds can be exchanged at par for the stock, and since one bond equals five shares of stock, the value of the debentures will follow upward the value of the stock for which they can be exchanged. So much for the profit side of the speculation. Any one holding the bond will see it rise in value as the stock rises.

But, as we have seen, there is a loss side to speculation, a side nearly always in evidence. And it is these losses which speculation, through the purchase of convertible debentures, will reduce to a minimum. In the case just cited, suppose net earnings fall 50 per cent., due to an industrial depression. The price of the stock purchased at 90, when a 6 per cent. dividend was paid, might fall to 45, when the payment of dividends, owing to reduced earnings, was suspended. Suppose now that, with $5,000 cash, our speculator had purchased 550 shares on a 10 per cent. margin. In the decline, if he held on and did not sell, his $5,000 would soon be gone. But if he had bought on the same margin 50 convertible debenture bonds at 100, he might have a chance.

For these debentures come ahead of the stock. Their interest must be paid before any dividends are paid. A decline in earnings which might make it necessary to pass a dividend need not affect the security of these debentures. They might not fall below 92. The speculator who held them might have to raise another $2,500 of margin. He might be forced to sell a part of his holdings to get the necessary margin to protect the remainder, but his loss need not be total. So long as interest on the debentures is earned, the fear of bankruptcy to follow the non-payment of interest will constrain the directors to protect the bonds. So the price of the debentures, as I have said, will not get down to 90, although the stock might fall to 45 or even lower.

Another method may be suggested whereby the spice of speculation may be injected into the nourishing but less appetizing dish of investment. This is the instalment plan of purchasing stocks. By this method, assuming that in three years you can save $15,000, and that you consider a certain stock, Erie 2d preferred, for example, an attractive purchase at 40. You believe, from study or advice, that within three years Erie 2d preferred will go to $70 per share. You want to profit by your conviction, to make the largest possible profit consistent with safety. You want to invest in Erie 2d preferred on margin, but you do not want to risk the loss of your capital. Assume that you have $1,500 to start with, and that you can save

$13,500 more in three years, at the rate of $375 a month. You make a contract with your broker to buy 375 shares of Erie 2d preferred at $40 a share, $1,500 down, and $375 a month for 36 months. When the broker makes this contract with you, you are safe against being sold out, so long as you keep your agreement. Erie 2d preferred may drop to 30 the day after the contract is signed, but the broker must hold the stock for you and deliver it to you when you pay $13,500, either in the instalments stipulated or in larger sums.

Now suppose the Goddess of Chance, not being able to get at you, sheltered behind your instalment contract, to do you harm, turns propitious and Erie goes up to 50 the month after your contract is signed. You have more than doubled your money, for you can sell your 375 shares for $18,750, pay your broker the $13,500 you owe him, plus commission and interest, and have about $3,500 in place of your original $1,500. If this method is applied to the purchase of dividend-paying stocks which will produce an income to offset the interest, stocks which have a solid basis in assets and earnings, and which you would be glad to hold as permanent investments, there is no valid criticism to be made against it.

II

STOCKS OR BONDS

WE turn now from the subject of speculation, the purchase or sale of securities to make a profit from their rise or fall, to the subject of investment, the purchase of securities to receive the interest or dividends which they pay, and the first question which we encounter is the choice of securities. Shall the investor buy stocks or bonds?

"Give me a seat in the front row," said an investor to his banker. "No stock, no real estate, no equities, for me. I do not want to look over the shoulders of the audience. I want the front row. Put my money into bonds."

This is the richest nation in the world, and, next to France, the most thrifty. In a normal year the net income of the American people, after paying most liberal living expenses, is far in excess of their operating expenses. An enormous amount remains for investment. What becomes of this money? A large amount of this money is put into savings banks. A large amount goes into insurance. A still larger sum is put into enterprises of various kinds which have stock for sale. Some goes into real estate, and a constantly increasing fraction into bonds.

It has been estimated that on the average a quarter of a billion dollars a year, and the real figures are probably higher, is lost in bad investments; sunk in margins on the stock exchange; donated to the brood of mining and industrial schemes whose promises are gold, and whose performances are chaff and stubble; invested in town lots in some "thriving industrial suburb"; or even used to purchase on margin standard railway and industrial stocks, which seem to advance only long enough to inflict heavy losses upon those who purchase them for still further gains. These are the vast losses in the game of business hazard, where the dice are always loaded and the cards are always marked.

On the other hand are the timid ones, who buy the obligations of the government, who put their money into savings banks or into life insurance, whose most daring flights are the purchases of the homes in which they live. These are recruited either from the anæmic or the dyspeptic, or from the burnt children who, as a result of sad experience, dread the fire. Between these two classes are the institutional buyers of bonds; the insurance companies; savings and commercial banks, who purchase as trustees for their policy-holders and depositors, taking a liberal toll for their service; and the individual bond-buyer, the man who is intelligent enough to buy his investments at first hand, and, at the same time, sufficiently conservative to decline to participate in the risks of business.

"What is a bond? How does it differ from a share of stock? Why does it offer a safer place for my savings than a savings bank or a trust company, while at the same time allowing me a moderate share in the profits of business?" These are questions often heard, but seldom clearly answered.

A bond is a promissory note, a contract to pay money, executed and issued by a corporation, either public or engaged in private business, and bearing interest at 4, 5, or 6 per cent., according to the location of the borrowing company or the business in which the corporation is engaged. The payment of this promissory note is usually secured, principal and interest, by a second agreement, executed between the borrowing company and a trustee for the lender, usually a trust company, by which the property of the buyer is transferred to the trustee, in trust, to secure the punctual performance by the corporation of all its agreements, including not merely the payment of interest and of principal when the note matures, but the keeping of the property in good repair, and the performance of many other covenants which increase the safety of the loan. The corporation bond is, therefore, not only protected like any other promissory note by all the property of the borrower which can be sold for the lender's benefit if default is made on either interest or principal, but it is safer than an unsecured promissory note in that the property of the borrower is formally set aside as security for the loan. The borrowing company can neither sell the property nor place any additional incumbrance upon it, nor increase the amount of its indebtedness secured by existing incumbrances, without the consent of every bondholder, which is, of course, seldom given.

And this is not all. If only the bonds of "going concerns" are purchased—that is, the bonds of corporations doing a profitable and increasingly prosperous business—the security of the investor whose bonds are protected by a first lien on all the property of the corporation, is not merely the property which is purchased with the money which he pays for his bonds, and which he is safe in supposing will earn more than enough to pay his interest, but, in addition, all the previously existing property of the company. In other words, if the investor exercises that degree of care in the selection of his bonds which any prudent man will naturally give to the conduct of affairs in which he is interested, both his principal and his interest are secured and secure.

Now contrast the position of the corporation bond-holder, the creditor of the company, with the position of the stock-holder. A share of stock is a certificate of part ownership in a corporation. A corporation is an association of persons to which the law gives the right, after certain simple formalities have been complied with, to own property, and to carry on certain kinds of business. It is the association which owns the property, which borrows, buys, and sells. The association issues stock which represents its ownership, in exchange for money or property.

This stock is divided into shares. It comes into possession of those who expect through its means to share in the profits of the company. The stock-holder is the owner of the corporation, as the corporation is the owner of the property. The stockholder does not own any part of the factory, or mine, or railroad. He owns a part of the company, and the company owns the property.

As the stock-holder does not own the property of his company, so he does not manage the company's business. That is done for him by trustees called directors, whom the law makes him elect. Each share of stock counts as one vote at the election, and a majority of the stock can elect the entire board. For example, a corporation capitalized at $10,000,000 may have 100,000 shares of stock. An investor has purchased 100 shares. At the election he has 100 votes out of 100,000, or one thousandth part of the total. So the "right to vote," which is one of the privileges of the stock-holder, not enjoyed by the bond-holder, amounts to little.

The small stock-holders in the best managed, largest, and soundest American corporations, either singly or in combination, have, practically speaking, no influence upon the election of directors. Where the officers care to take the trouble they may send out proxies, blank powers of attorney for stock-holders to sign, but in only the most exceptional cases can an individual stock-holder, who has, in theory, the same right to solicit proxies as the officers, gain sufficient support to influence the election.

So well is this powerlessness of the stock-holder recognized, that some of the largest railway systems in the United States are dominated down to the last director and the last official by men who own only a few shares of stock, but who, in case of need, can secure by sending out requests for proxies, the coöperation of a sufficient number of stock-holders to enable them to control a disputed election. The late Henry O. Havemeyer, who was in absolute control of the American Sugar Refining Company to the day of his death, held about 2/100 of one per cent. of its stock when he passed away. Elections are seldom disputed. Stock-holders are too widely scattered and too apathetic to take much interest in the way their company's affairs are conducted. While they receive dividends, they are content, and when dividends are reduced or suspended, their dissatisfaction seldom rises above sleepy growls of irritation and disgust.

The stock-holder also has the right to participate in profits, when, and only when, these are distributed by the Board of Directors. If the profits are not earned, he receives no dividends.

Even when large profits have been earned, he cannot obtain any share in them, unless the directors declare a dividend, and there is no power to force the directors to take such action. They can decide to pile up profits, and the stock-holders, unless they are able to put the directors out, which seldom happens, are helpless to interfere. They own shares in the company, it is true, but often this does them little good.

Of course, there is a brighter side to the picture. Sometimes profits are very large, and the stock-holder gets large dividends, but he must always bear in mind that the bond-holder's interest must first be paid, and that any losses which the company may sustain must first fall upon its owners. And how numerous those losses are! Within a few months in 1908, the United States plunged from prosperity into depression, and down went the dividends of many of the strongest railroads and industries; some of them suspended altogether, others seriously reduced.

The stock-holder has no assurance, moreover, that the amount of stock outstanding will remain where it is. He may be called upon to authorize a doubling of the capital stock, raising the number of shares from 100,000 to 200,000. The new stock may be issued for property or for money, and the investment may be profitable, but there are now twice as many shares, and the universal practice of increasing stock capital keeps down the dividend rates of even the most prosperous companies to 6 or 7 per cent.

It is a hard saying, but a true one, that the small stock-holder in American business corporations has no influence in selecting the directors, no voice in the management, and but little power to protect himself against the directors should they decide to keep him out of his profits for the purpose of depressing the value of his holdings, so that they may purchase it from him at low figures, or practice upon him sundry other arts of the stock manipulator. He is powerless to prevent an unlimited increase in the amount of stock, if made for lawful purposes and in a lawful manner. He has no claim upon the company to pay him dividends, and if he is dissatisfied with the way his business is conducted, his only remedy, in the language of a famous legal decision, is either "to elect new directors"—a manifest impossibility for the small investor—or "to sell his stock and withdraw," which he frequently does at a considerable discount from the price he paid.

STOCKS OR BONDS

How different and how vastly superior is the position of the investor who has purchased from reputable and responsible bankers the mortgage bonds of the same enterprises whose stock-holders are liable to so many hardships and mishaps. In common with the stock-buyer, the bond-buyer contributes money to construct and extend the plant of the corporation. They are both interested in its property and its profits. But here the resemblance between the position of the two investors abruptly ends. The bond-holder must be paid his interest regularly or the company becomes a bankrupt. The stock-holder's dividends need not be paid at all, unless the directors so decide, and they may be lowered or raised at the directors' pleasure. There is no certainty about them.

The bond-holder knows that his money has gone into some kind of property—his trustee sees to that. The stock of the same company may have been originally issued for the "good-will"—often the "good will" of those who receive the stock. The money which he pays very often goes not to the company, but to its promoters, and those who have sold property to it. The money which is paid for stock takes the forms, not of rails, ties, and power-houses, but of automobiles, horses and yachts. The bond-holder does not own any part of the corporation, as does the stock-holder, but, on the other hand, the stock-holder does not control any part of the property, while all the property is conveyed to a trustee for the safeguarding of the bond-holder's interests. The bond-holder knows how much of a particular issue he owns, and he knows that the total amount of this debt may not be increased unless he gives his consent. Before the stock-holder, on the other hand, stretches an endless vista of new issues, whose amount he is powerless to regulate or limit.

The bond-holder has a first claim upon earnings. In very few cases will they ever fall so far as to endanger his interest. Even in those cases where bonds of inferior security, or which have been issued in excessive amounts, are purchased without proper investigation, from bankers who valued immediate profits above the permanent confidence of satisfied customers—and most of these bankers belong to a past generation—and when these bonds have been in default, the investor has seldom suffered any permanent damage if he has held on to his security. These companies have been reorganized; new bonds or preferred stock are issued for the bonds in default; and, in the great majority of cases, all the losses have been regained, sometimes with a large profit. The stock-holder, on the other hand, takes what is left after interest is paid, be that remainder much or little. He comes after the bond-holder. He sits in the lowest room, eats at the second table, occupies a seat in the back row. Long before the bond-holder's interest is reached by the decline in earnings, the stock-holder's dividends are suspended, and the reorganization which passes lightly over the creditors falls upon the owners with crushing force.

As a final difference between stock and bonds, the value of a first mortgage bond, because of all the advantages and points of superiority which have been mentioned, changes very little in comparison with the value of the stock of the same company. The stocks of even the safest and best managed companies show the most astonishing gyrations, the wildest fluctuations. They fall $10, $20, $30, $50, a share, within a few months, while the bonds, securely protected by their position as first and fixed claimants to income, rise and fall very slowly and within very narrow limits. The owner can usually be certain of realizing on his investment with but trifling loss. What the stock-holder will get may depend on the honesty of some New York bank president, the digestion of a high government officer or the success of the advertising campaign of some stock-manipulator. Whether to sell or to pledge as security for loans, bonds are conspicuously better than stocks.

Now, then, if bonds are so much better than stocks, that the wayfaring man, if not altogether a fool, cannot fail to appreciate their superiority, how shall bonds be bought? Shall the investor turn his money over to an insurance company in an "endowment" policy, or to a savings bank or trust company, or shall he buy bonds direct? The answer is not difficult. It is his money which buys the bonds in any event, whether he deposits it in a bank or pays it as premiums to an insurance company, or whether he chooses the better plan, and himself buys the same bonds which these institutions purchase with the money which he contributes.

Why should he not buy direct and obtain the higher interest of direct ownership? There is only one objection to direct bond-buying, the lack of the ability, or rather the lack of experience, of the private investor to select sound investments. There are all sorts of bonds, good, bad, and indifferently poor. Great care and much intelligent investigation is required to choose good bonds for investment. The insurance companies and the savings banks pay high salaries to experienced men to make investments for these institutions. Their depositors and policy-holders reap the benefit in perfect security, to obtain which they sacrifice a part of the money which is earned on the investment of their money by these institutions. The investor does not possess this ability. Left to himself in his bond-buying, he may go badly astray. Nor can he afford to pay adequate fees to expert advisers.

Into this situation comes the bond-house, with its organization of experienced investigators, far superior to those employed by the insurance company or savings bank, its large capital and still larger credit. The bond-house buys the bonds of enterprises in which it has confidence with its own money, purchasing them not as a broker or agent, but as an investor, and then resells them at a small profit to private investors, who are in this way able to purchase, with perfect security in both interest and principal, bonds which pay them much higher returns than they can receive from any institution to which they may entrust their savings.

III

THE CORPORATION MORTGAGE AND THE DEED OF TRUST

MOST people who have saved money are acquainted with the nature of a mortgage. They understand it as a lien upon property, given to secure a debt. The conditions of the lien are that, in case the debt is not paid at maturity, the lender who holds the lien can force a sale of the property by judicial process, having his own debt paid out of the proceeds, and returning any balance to the borrower.

While the operation and effect of the real-estate mortgage are generally familiar, the nature of the lien conferred by the mortgage is not equally well understood. A mortgage is a conveyance of property by the owner to the lender. It is in form and in effect a deed similar to the ordinary deed by which property is conveyed from one person to another. The conveyance is, however, coupled with the condition that the creditor holds the title to the property, as trustee for the owner. The conditions of the trust are as follows. If the debt to secure which the conveyance is made is not paid at maturity, or if any other covenant in the mortgage is broken by the lender, the trust, which up to that time has been a "passive" trust, becomes active, and the lender, known as the mortgagee, asserts his title to the property and forces its sale.

The agreement between the parties binds the borrower, the owner of the property, not only to the payment of interest and principal, but also to the performance of certain other covenants of great importance to the security of the debt. For example, the owner must insure the property and make the policies payable to the lender; he must also pay the taxes and deliver the tax receipts to the holder of the mortgage, since a failure to pay taxes might result in a sale of the property by the State, which would deprive the lender of his security. The borrower agrees to keep the property in good repair. He further agrees not to sell any portion of the mortgaged property without the consent of the lender, who will, of course, not allow such a sale to be made unless the proceeds are applied either to the liquidation of the debt or to the purchase of new property of equal value to that sold.

This mortgage or conditional deed which conveys the title to real property to the lender is given to secure a debt in the form of a bond. This bond is a simple promise to pay a definite sum of money, with interest, at a certain date in the future. It is signed by the owner of the property. The real-estate mortgage therefore comprises two contracts: first, a contract to pay money, and, second, a conveyance of real estate to secure the fulfilment of a contract to pay money.

When the conveyance, otherwise known as the mortgage, is copied into a book of record kept in a public office for the inspection of all those who may be interested, it fixes the title of the mortgage-holder as against all the world. The owner of the property, who is left in possession so long as he carries out his agreements with the lender, is free to sell his interest in the property. He must sell it, however, subject to the right of the lender to enforce the provisions of his contract. It is impossible, in any other way than by a tax sale, to separate the interest of the lender from the property to which that interest attaches.

We have these principles carried out in the corporation mortgage bond, the universal form of safe investment. There is, first, a promise to pay $1,000,000, $5,000,000, or $100,000,000 in ten, twenty, or fifty years from date. This promise to pay, executed by the officers of the corporation, is not expressed in the form of a single note, but is divided into 1,000, 10,000, or 100,000 notes, numbered serially from one to the total number, and all identical in form, with the single difference in the numbers. This division of the corporate debt into "pieces" is for purposes of convenience in marketing. It is unusual for one investor to take more than a small portion of a large loan. By dividing a large debt into a number of identical notes, each of small denomination, it is possible for the company to make a wide distribution of its bonds and gather funds from a great number of private investors and institutions.

Just as the corporation bond differs but slightly from the bonds executed in connection with the real-estate mortgage, so the corporation mortgage is practically identical with the more familiar real-estate mortgage. Because the creditors of the corporation are numerous, it is impossible to make the conveyance to the lenders—there are too many lenders. It is necessary, therefore, that a trustee should be appointed to act for the lenders, and to hold the property in trust for the securing of these various obligations. Sometimes an individual trustee is named for this purpose. The usual practice, however, is to designate a trust company, which, because of its large capital, and its administrative organization experienced in the conduct of matters of this kind, makes a more satisfactory trustee than an individual. A corporation mortgage is, therefore, usually known as a deed of trust, or sometimes as a mortgage deed of trust.

The form of the corporation deed of trust follows the usual outline of real-estate mortgages. There is first a description of the bond to secure which the mortgage is executed. Then comes the detailed description of the property. This property is next conveyed to the trustee in a form of which the following is a type:

NOW, THEREFORE, THIS INDENTURE WITNESS-ETH that, for and in consideration of the premises and of the acceptance of the refunding bonds by the holders thereof, and of the sum of one hundred dollars, lawful money of the United States of America, to it duly paid by the Trustee at or before the ensealing and delivery of these presents, the receipt whereof is hereby acknowledged, and for other good and valuable considerations, Rogers-Brown Iron Company has granted, bargained, sold, aliened, remised, released, conveyed, confirmed, assigned, transferred and set over, and by these presents does grant, bargain, sell, alien, remise, release, convey, confirm, assign, transfer and set over unto the Trustee, its successors in the trust and its and their assigns, forever, all and singular the following described or mentioned property, rights and franchises, which collectively are hereinafter generally called the trust estate, to wit:

Then follows a detailed description of the property, the same description that is contained in the original deeds by which the borrowing and pledging corporation took title to the various properties named in the mortgage.

The nature of the conveyance is, however, not absolute, but conditional. This appears in the following clause; respectively called the Habendum Clause and the Grant in Trust:

TO HAVE AND TO HOLD all and singular the said property, rights and franchises unto the Trustee, its successors in the trust and its and their assigns, forever:—

IN TRUST, NEVERTHELESS, for the equal and proportionate benefit and security of all holders and registered owners of refunding bonds and coupons and, . . . for the enforcement of the payment of the principal . . . and interest of all such bonds when payable, according to the tenor, purport and effect of such bonds and coupons, and to secure the performance and observance of and compliance with the covenants and conditions of this indenture, without preference, priority, or distinction as to lien or otherwise of one bond over any other bond by reason of priority in the issue, sale or negotiation thereof . . . and so that the principal, premium and interest of every such bond shall, subject to the terms hereof, be equally and proportionately secured hereby as if all had been duly issued, secured, and negotiated simultaneously with the execution and delivery hereof.

Up to this point, there is no substantial difference to be observed between the wording of the real-estate mortgage and the wording of the corporate mortgage. The only points of variance of the corporation mortgage are the greater complexity, and the fact that in the corporation mortgage the conveyance is not to the lender direct, but to the lender's representative.

From this point, however, the corporate mortgage differs from the real-estate mortgage in that it contains a variety of covenants entered into by the company which owns the property, with the trustee who holds the property in trust for the security of the debt. These covenants are calculated to maintain the value of the security.

In addition to a repetition of the agreements contained in the bond to pay principal and interest, the company which owns the property agrees with the trustee in the mortgage that it will pay the taxes; that it will pay all claims for labor and materials out of which mechanic's liens might arise, which might precede the claim of the trustee to the property; that the company will maintain the property in good condition and repair, and will continue to operate the property in the conduct of the business to which it is specifically devoted, as, for example, the production of pig iron or the business of transportation; that any property which they may thereafter acquire, they will, by supplementary deeds, convey to the trustee as additional security to that already conveyed; that they will not, without the consent of the trustee, sell any portion of the property, and that this consent will be given only on condition that the proceeds of the sale represent a fair price for the property disposed of, and that these proceeds are invested in new property to take the place of that withdrawn; that the company will keep all property subject to the danger of fire damage fully insured, and that, if the trustee desires, the policies of insurance shall be made payable to the order of the trustee, so that the money will come into his hands, in order that he may superintend its disbursement; that, in so far as the company operates any franchises granted by municipalities, the obligations of these franchises will be faithfully observed; that, in so far as it holds any property under lease, it will faithfully carry out the covenants of these leases; and, in general, that the company executing the mortgage and owning the property will carefully conserve and protect the physical condition and the value of the business as a going concern, so that the bond-holders may have at all times adequate security for their debt.

The mortgage also prescribes the method of

enforcing the rights of the bond-holders in case of default in principal or interest, or the breach of any other covenant in the mortgage. In such an event, the trustee is sometimes authorized to seize the property and operate it for the benefit of the bond-holders, or, failing in this, to proceed in the manner prescribed by law to have the property sold and the proceeds of the sale applied to the liquidation of the debt. This mortgage is then recorded in the county seat of every county in which the property covered by the mortgage may be located. From the date of recording until every covenant in the mortgage has been discharged, the bonds of the company are protected by a lien upon the property from which this property can in no way be released.

It has been noted that the lien of the mortgage has been treated as a lien upon property. In the case of a mortgage given by a business corporation, the security is, however, far more than the physical property. This physical property is operated by a business organization which often represents the result of many years' careful work on the part of the owners, and which has reached a high degree of efficiency. Connected with the property is also a certain amount of prestige and good-will, a business reputation which brings trade and increases profits. All of these assets—physical property, business organization, good-will—together represent the earning power of the company, its ability to produce a profit. In these profits, not only because the company has promised to pay him money, but because that promise to pay is backed up by a conveyance of all the physical property of the company, the bond-holder, after the claim of the State for taxes, has the first right to share.

The mortgage bond-holder is more than a creditor of the company. His rights do not depend merely upon his ability to sue the company in case of default in principal or interest, and collect from it by the ordinary process of law. This right to sue and collect is a valuable one, but the mortgage bond-holder can go much further than this. He is also an owner, through his trustee, of the property of the company. He has an interest in that property. Although that interest is held in trust for him, yet should need arise, the powers of the trust can be asserted, and the property can be seized and sold for his benefit.

It is this feature of ownership which so sharply distinguishes the position of the stock-holder from that of the mortgage bond-holder. The stock-holder has merely an interest in the company. He owns no property. He and his fellow stock-holders, it is true, own the company, and the company owns the property subject to the ownership of the bond-holder. This is a very different thing from the direct ownership of the property, which is enjoyed by the bond-holder. Through his trustee, the bond-holder actually owns the property. The claim of the stock-holder for dividends is contingent not merely upon these dividends being earned, but upon the decision of the directors to distribute the earnings to the owners of the company. With the bond-holder's rights, however, the directors can take no liberties. He bears a more direct relation to the trust estate than do the stock-holders. They are continued in possession only so long as they perform the covenants of the mortgage. The bond-holders are the owners of the property, and they will assert their title through the trustee if the company does not faithfully and regularly pay them their interest.

IV

THE BANKING HOUSE AS AN AID TO INVESTORS

THE plan followed by the conservative invest-ment-banker in offering bonds to his customers is, first, to purchase the bonds himself, and thus to evidence his faith in their soundness. The expression "We own and offer" is frequently met with in bankers' literature. Before purchasing any bond from a banking house, the investor should be careful to ascertain that the house is not acting as the agent or representative of the actual owners.

The risk which the banker takes is not so great as that assumed by his customer, since an enterprise may be entirely sound in its early stages, when its bonds are sold to the investor, and may be afterwards wrecked by bad management. This risk the banker passes on to his customer. The customer must rely upon the banker's anxiety to maintain the good-will of his business, to protect him from purchasing unsound securities.

Notwithstanding this transference of the risk, the banker must assume it in the first instance, and cases are not lacking where large issues of bonds have been purchased with the idea of reselling them to the investor, but which, by reason of some miscalculation on the banker's part, could not be sold at a profit and were left on his hands.

Before purchasing any issue of bonds, therefore, the conservative investment-banker will provide for a careful investigation of every feature of the proposition upon the basis of which the bonds are issued.

The countless disappointments in the development of new enterprises are mainly due to faulty investigation as to the possibilities of the project, which leads to wrong conclusions as to the profits which will be earned. It is the business of the banker to guard against these mistakes. The consideration of a few typical cases will show how serious is the risk of the investor who purchases securities the soundness of which has not been determined by an exhaustive preliminary investigation.

In the neighborhood of a large Eastern city, there is a suburban electric railroad, running out about twelve miles from a terminal station at the end of a city transportation line, through a number of fashionable suburban towns, parallelling throughout this entire distance the main line of a large and well managed steam-railway company, particularly distinguished for the excellence of its suburban passenger service. The syndicate which promoted this enterprise, and which completed it with its own money—no securities being offered to the public—employed engineers of high reputation and sound attainments to examine into the cost and anticipated traffic of the enterprise. The line was surveyed, estimates were made of the cost of obtaining ground for a right-of-way, and arrangements were made to purchase a large amount of real estate for the development of suburban towns which would furnish traffic to the line.

The engineers then addressed themselves to the possibilities of traffic for the new line. These engineers had obtained their experience in the West where the interurban electric railway has developed in competition with the steam roads, and where experience has shown that the electric line will almost invariably draw a certain percentage of the traffic of the steam line, which will be attracted by the lower rates and more frequent service. The method followed in the West in figuring the traffic of a proposed electric line, is carefully to estimate the traffic of the steam line with which it is to compete, and to take a certain percentage of the number of passengers as the share of the electric line, adding thereto an estimate of the new traffic which the electric line will develop.

In the case under examination, the engineers followed this method. They made a careful computation of the traffic at each of the stations on the line of railroad which their line was to parallel, and from this estimate, allowing for a certain amount of new business, they computed the traffic which would be gained by the suburban line. Their estimates were accepted by the syndicate, and over three million dollars was provided for construction and the purchase of land.

No sooner was the line put into operation, however, than it was found that the engineers had made serious blunders in their calculations. The people of the towns through which the new line ran were entirely satisfied with the service furnished them by the steam line. The trains were frequent and were seldom crowded. Passengers were delivered at a station in the centre of the city. The new suburban line, on the other hand, could give them only connection with the city line, necessitating a change of cars, which was inconvenient. The residents of these towns were, for the most part, well to do. The advantages of saving a few cents in their fare did not particularly appeal to them; neither did the more frequent service offered by the electric line prove much of an inducement, since the bulk of the traffic was hauled at the beginning and end of the day. As a consequence, the traffic of the new line proved a sore disappointment to the promoters. It failed from the beginning to pay its fixed charges, and for a considerable time even its operating expenses were not earned. It has since been sold at less than one-third of the amount of money invested in its construction; an expensive extension has been built to make it profitable; and the original syndicate has suffered a heavy loss.

Another case related to a water-power enterprise in a Southern State. The original estimates of the cost of construction in this case were $1,900,000, but these estimates were so radically defective that when the project was about half completed the money was exhausted. The property was placed in the hands of a receiver, who, on the basis of expert engineering investigation, estimated that over $1,500,000 would be required to complete the project. The promoting syndicate was forced to sell the half completed plant at a heavy sacrifice, and it has since been completed by another company.

Mr. H. M. Byllesby, the Chicago engineer, in a recent address on the securities of water-power companies as investments, mentions the following instance as an example of the great danger of underestimating the cost of new enterprises: "In developing a large and very necessary reservoir, they made some soundings (but not enough), they dug some test pits (but not enough), and located what they believed to be a rock ledge, upon which they have begun to build a dam to impound the water in the reservoir; and now, after having closed the door for the raising of further funds, they find themselves in an extremely embarrassing position, because, contrary to all geological data at their command, contrary to the showing of their test pits, this ledge of rock, instead of drifting uniformly across the gorge where the dam is being built, has developed a 'fault' at the centre, of unknown depth, and which can only be bridged over or made safe by the expenditure of about twenty-five per cent. of the cost of the project. If it were not for the fact that the men back of this enterprise have large individual personal means and ample credit, the raising of this additional money . . . would probably force this particular enterprise to a drastic reorganization."

In cases like the above, and they are numerous, mistakes in estimates are made, some unavoidable, but most of which could have been prevented by the employment of good engineers. If the investor buys securities offered on behalf of a new company, he is almost certain to buy into the effects of some such blunders as I˙ have indicated. The banking house, on the contrary, takes pains to avoid such mistakes by making an investigation of the proposition, an investigation so thorough and so searching that no important defect will be left undisclosed.

The following is an outline of the method of investigation employed by a prominent banking house when requested to purchase an issue of corporation securities:

This house is averse to purchasing so-called "unseasoned" or construction bonds. An enterprise may be never so promising in prospect, and yet, if it has no established record of earnings, no balance sheet and income account to present, if its earnings are still on paper, this house will refuse to have anything to do with it.

THE CAREFUL INVESTOR

New enterprises are best promoted and financed by construction syndicates. Banking houses may take an interest in these syndicates as promoters, expecting to make a portion of the promoters' profits; they may invite some of their own customers into the syndicate, not as investors, but as promoters like themselves; but they will take good care that the enterprise has passed the construction stage, that a full fiscal year has been completed, and that a comfortable margin over interest charges is shown by the income account, before they make any public offering of the bonds.

Even when bonds are seasoned, however, they will not be offered until the condition of the company issuing them has been subjected to an exhaustive analysis. The owners are first requested to submit complete data regarding the company, which are analyzed in the office of the banking concern. If no weakness is disclosed, such, for example, as stationary population, or too high a percentage of interest charges to gross earnings, the formal examination begins. First comes the examination of the engineer. Only expert engineers of long experience and high reputation, men qualified by familiarity with corporations of the class under examination, are employed. The engineer's examination goes into the condition of the property, the character of the management, the adequacy of the rates charged to the customers, the relations between the company and its employees, the physical value of the corporation's property, and the chances of growth in the community in which it operates.

Next comes the audit of the corporation's accounts. Many banking houses employ their own auditors for this purpose. In the absence of such a skilled employee, they rely upon the advice of outside accountants of standing and experience. The object of the audit is to see, first, that the accounts are so kept that they show the actual condition of the company, and second, to determine whether, for example, such items as the cost of power or the cost of maintenance are abnormally high.

The banking house also insists upon a careful legal investigation. This relates primarily to the franchises under which the company is given the right, for a term of years, to use public property for its own purposes. The banker's attorney will make sure that these franchises are sufficiently broad for the purposes of the company; that they do not impose burdensome restrictions; that they run for a sufficient time to enable the business to be properly developed; and that they contain satisfactory provisions for renewal at their expiration.

The attorney also gives much thought to the preparation of the mortgage under which the property of the company is conveyed to the trustee for the securing of its bonds. The mortgage will set forth, in great detail, the property which is transferred. It will bind the company by stringent provisions to maintain the value of this security intact, and it will carefully limit and safeguard the future issues of bonds secured by the same mortgage, so that a large margin of security in the cost of the property will be assured to the bond-holders.

If, after this investigation, the banker is convinced that the bonds are safe; and that their safety will so increase that any one buying these bonds will be assured of a fixed income for a term of years, and the return of his principal at the end of the term, the banker will purchase the bonds, and will then offer them to his customers.

The investor has none of the equipment for

making an investigation of this kind. If he relies upon the representations of the promoters of any scheme, he is almost certain to be misled. If he attempts to investigate the proposition for himself, his failure is likely to be both ludicrous and lamentable. If, however, he relies upon the recommendations of a banking house of standing, there is little chance of his losing his money.

V

THE BUSINESS OF THE INVESTMENT-BANKER

In the field of security investments, the buyer should seek information on three points: (1) Shall I purchase stocks or bonds? (2) From whom shall I purchase my securities? (3) In what industries shall I invest? The first question was answered in the last chapter. We have now to take up the second question: From whom shall I purchase my bonds?

The security business, in its organization, resembles any other business. There are the manufacturers, the companies which issue the bonds; the distributors—investment-bankers, investment or finance companies, savings-bank and insurance companies, which purchase bonds from the producers, and, directly or indirectly, place them in the hands of the consumer; and finally the consumer, the investor, the policy-holder, or the savings-bank depositor. In the field of merchandise distribution, there are some producers who deal directly with the consumer, but these are the exceptions. Generally speaking, the producers of shoes, hats, groceries, and drygoods have found it economical, and in all other ways satisfactory, to deal with the wholesaler. The jobber will buy in round lots from the manufacturer, taking his entire season's output of a certain line, assuring him his money without risk or trouble of collection, and enabling him to make his financial and industrial plans on a basis of assured receipts.

It is even more advantageous for the manufacturer of bonds, the borrowing company, to deal with the bond-jobber, the investment-banker. The investment-banker is in most cases a partnership. If of the first rank, the concern will have a large capital, and a credit with banks and trust companies several times the amount of its capital. The investment-banker will also have associations with other houses of the same kind, which will place at his disposal large sums of cash whenever he requires. The business of the investment-banker is the purchase and sale of securities. He sometimes adds to this other functions similar to those performed by a commercial bank, such as receiving deposits subject to check, and the purchase and sale of bills of foreign exchange. His main business, however, is dealing in investment securities.

THE CAREFUL INVESTOR

The investment-banker, the jobber of bonds, organizes his business on the lines of a hardware or drygoods jobber. He has in his files the names of a large number, sometimes many thousands, of present, prospective, or potential customers. He knows about how much money each has to invest, and the approximate dates when this money is available. He has an organization of salesmen who visit these customers, impressing upon them the merits of the securities offered by their house. The work of the salesmen is supplemented by letters, circulars, and public advertising. Some of the large houses extend their operations to foreign countries. They can draw upon the investment resources of France, Holland, England, and Germany. The investment-banker sells largely to institutions—insurance companies, trust companies, state and national banks.

These security jobbers stand ready to purchase for cash the bonds and sometimes the stocks of corporations and municipalities. The prices which they offer the corporation are, of course, below the prices which they expect to receive—four points on some bonds, ten points on others. Out of the difference they pay their expenses and make their profit. It is nearly always advantageous for both the security producer (the corporation) and the security consumer (the investor) to deal with the security jobber.

To the corporation, the advantage of dealing with the investment-banker are evident. To begin with, when the contract with the banker is signed, the cost to the corporation of obtaining the money which it requires is determined. The bonds may be sold at 85, 87½, or 95. No matter what the price, the cost of the money is known. This money will be paid over to the corporation either at definite dates or on demand. Contracts can be made for cars, or locomotives, or bridge material, with absolute certainty that the money to pay the bills will be in hand.

The cost to the corporation of selling securities direct to investment-jobbers is usually much less than the cost by the alternative method of direct sale to the investor. The certainty of return, moreover, is far greater. The banker has a permanent organization and an established clientèle of customers. The organization is constantly at work marketing bonds and many of the customers are steadily buying. Most of the older houses control the security trade of a large part of their clientèle who will buy from no one else. The investment-banker can count on a certain amount of money from these customers at regular intervals.

It is not necessary for the banker to force his bonds on an unwilling market. By utilizing his credit, the banker can usually borrow up to 80 per cent. of the cost of these securities which they have purchased.

An established banking-house can also employ the method of trading a new issue for an old. Their regular customers, upon whom the bankers can rely to buy their quota of any new issue, may have purchased all the bonds they can pay for. They have, however, old bonds with established records of interest payments, so-called "seasoned" bonds, which are readily salable. The bonds of the new issue are now exchanged for the "seasoned" bonds on terms which show a profit to the holder of the old bonds. For example, he is allowed to buy a $1,000 bond which would cost him $950 in cash for $950 in old bonds. The old bonds thus acquired by the bankers can be sold perhaps for 97, although they might have difficulty in selling the new bonds at 93.

Finally, the investment-banker has the great advantage of associations in the same line of trade. Unlike the merchandise jobber, he has developed

to a high degree the methods of coöperative buying. When a new issue of bonds is to be purchased,
he can quickly form a purchasing syndicate containing perhaps twenty other houses, located in
all parts of the country. He has thus at his disposal twenty selling organizations and groups of
investors in addition to his own.

Sharply contrasted with the superior advantages
of the investment-banker as a distributor of securities, is the situation of the corporation which tries
to do this work for itself. A corporation engaged
in the mining of coal or the operation of an electric
railway does not possess any of the elaborate equipment necessary for the sale of large amounts of
securities on short notice. Since its demands for
new capital are occasional, dependent upon its
need for larger facilities, a company may run along
for five or six years without selling any securities.
There would be no occupation for a securities
selling department under these circumstances.
Any company, even a strong corporation, desiring
to sell bonds outside the circle of its own stock-
holders must construct a special organization for
the purpose and at the time. Such an organization is expensive and inefficient. The company
must rely on newspaper advertising to discover

its prospective customers, and this is a very expensive method.

Again, most companies have difficulty in borrowing from banks on the security of their own bonds, although the same security may be entirely satisfactory to the same banks when offered by the investment-banker. The cost of selling, and the proceeds of sale, under these conditions, would be equally uncertain. The corporation could not launch any extensive building programme, while relying upon so precarious a source from which to meet its contract obligations.

So important and so plain are the advantages of selling bonds to bankers instead of attempting to reach the investor direct, that the method of direct appeal is adopted only when necessity constrains. The manufacturer of shoes may decide to do without the jobber, and may establish his own chain of stores through which he may market his product direct. The wisdom of this method is doubtful as a general practice, but in a few cases it has undoubtedly succeeded. But the shoe-manufacturer is making shoes all the time. His factory runs continuously, if he can sell its output. His business is to manufacture and to sell shoes.

The manufacturer of railroad securities, however, only starts this portion of his productive machinery running when he needs money to build a new line, or to reduce grades, or to excavate tunnels, in order to reduce the cost of train movement. His business is to transport passengers and freight, not to make pig iron or cotton cloth. The raising of new capital by the sale of bonds or stocks is incidental and contributory to his main business. It is difficult to imagine a situation where it will be advantageous for a corporation, unless its own stock-holders are able to supply its need for new money, to offer its securities direct.

The conclusion, from the standpoint of the investor's interest, is plain. Whenever the investment-banker will buy, the corporation with bonds for sale will sell them to the investment-banker. Only when the banker will not purchase, or, as shown above, when the stock-holders of the company desiring to raise new capital are willing to add to their investment, will any other method than sale to the investment-banker be adopted. If, now, we find that the investment-banker will buy only the best bonds for sale to his clients, it is a safe conclusion that if the investor wishes good securities, he can rely upon getting them nowhere else than from the bankers whose business it is to select such securities and to sell them.

A moment's consideration of the case will suffice to show that the success of the investment-banker depends upon the quality of the bonds which he offers for sale. He expects his business to be permanent with every client. When a man has saved $1,000 and purchased a bond, it is a reasonable presumption, from the banker's standpoint, that he will repeat the operation many times, and the banker intends that, as far as possible, he shall supply the investments for the succeeding thousands also. Again, if the banker sells a bond maturing in ten or twenty years, he has a record of that sale, and when the bond is paid off he expects to have a new bond ready to take the place of the old one. He aims to cultivate, therefore, by every means in his power, the good-will of his customers. The number of investors, considered in relation to the total population, is small. Competition for their money is very keen. When once a prospect has been converted into a customer, the banker has the strongest possible motives of self-interest to keep him for a permanent customer.

The basis of the customer's good-will, the foundation upon which a large security-selling business must be erected, is the high quality, the impregnable security, of the bonds which the banking-house offers for sale. In his literature, in his advertisements, and through his salesmen, the banker lays strenuous emphasis upon the safety of his wares.. He recommends them to his customers. Usually he has bought them for himself before he offers them for sale. His constant endeavor is to protect his customers against loss. He will carry this solicitude for the customers' good-will so far, in some cases, as to repurchase bonds concerning whose value questions may have been raised, or whose reputation has been blown upon. He has been known to undertake, at his own risk, the work of reorganizing bankrupt companies whose bonds have passed through his hands, so that they may, without loss to the creditors, be started anew.

A man in such a business cannot afford to recommend to his customers bonds concerning whose soundness there may be any question. To depart from this rule means the ultimate destruction of his business. He may, as some bankers have done, sell a large amount of doubtful bonds or stocks during a period of business prosperity, when all enterprises, both bad and good, were making money. He may trade upon the confidence of his clients and temporarily enrich himself at their expense. But when a business depression overtakes these shaky enterprises which he has financed they go down in ruin, and with them goes the good-will of the banker's business.

We arrive, then, at this conclusion: since it is to the interest of corporations having bonds for sale to sell them through investment-bankers, and since it is to the interest of the investment-banker to purchase only safe bonds, it follows that safe bonds of new companies, those which are offered at attractive prices, can be purchased, as a rule, only through the investment-banker.

VI

THE RELIABLE INVESTMENT-BANKER

THE question is often asked, Does the investment-banker guarantee the securities that he sells? His literature abounds with assurances that any one who purchases his wares will not lose. The investment-banker, by his own representations, deals in securities. Whoever intrusts his money to him may sleep soundly, undisturbed by fears of loss. These representations are, moreover, true. Only a small, almost negligible fraction of the bonds placed through banking-houses of the first class are ever in trouble.

Still, losses and defaults sometimes occur. I have before me a circular letter addressed to the bond-holders of a manufacturing concern, now in receivers' hands, by a protective committee, inviting deposit of bonds for mutual defense and protection. The St. Louis and San Francisco bond-holders are making similar appeals. Such cases of default are fortunately rare. They do occur, however, and the investor who is thinking about the purchase of bonds will do well to have them in mind. By electing to take a bond rather than a share of stock, the investor has abandoned all claim to share in the profits of the business above the five or six per cent. which will be paid to him as interest. He has decided to choose safety of principal and a fixed income. He wishes some guarantee and assurance that his principal will be safe and his income secure. Can the investment-banker give him this assurance?

On some points the investor can feel satisfied, provided he deals only with banking-houses of proved reputation. He can be sure that, barring the "acts of God and the public enemy," his investment will be safe, that his interest will be paid him regularly, and that when his bond matures the money will be ready. If war or revolution destroys his investment, if fire, flood, earthquake, or tornado falls upon the property which secures his bonds, he may suffer a partial or total loss. Short of such calamities, however, which no foresight can anticipate, against which no forethought can provide, the conservative investment banker can assure his customers absolute protection.

He can give them this assurance because he has thoroughly investigated the security of the bonds which he sells. He has satisfied himself that all legal safeguards are thrown about the borrower, that the physical condition of the property is sound, that the total bond-issue is less than the replacement value of the property, that the earnings are well above the interest charges, that the management is capable and progressive, and that the demand for the product or service—the gas, or water, or electricity, or transportation—which the company is organized to furnish, is reasonably certain to increase. By the banker's investigation, every unknown factor has been eliminated. He is offering certainties to his customers; he sells them a secured income and a secured return of principal.

But still one question has not been answered. What is the backing of these assurances? What guaranty does the banker give that his representations and his promises will be borne out by the result? If you purchase a house, you apply for title insurance. For a small fee, a trust company places its surplus and capital back of your title. It gives you absolute assurance that you will suffer no damage from any defect in your title. Does the investment-banker give the same assurance?

Suppose, for example, that you buy $5,000 bonds

secured by a mortgage on a trolley system, and that, after a few years, your interest fails to be paid. A receiver is appointed for the property. A reorganization plan is offered the bond-holders. What, then, will be the attitude of the banker who sold you the bonds? Will he make good your loss, or will he cite to you the ancient proverb, the swindler's city of refuge, *"Caveat Emptor"* (Let the buyer beware)? Is the banker's guaranty worth anything? Has it substance? Granted that it is only a moral guaranty, will the banker make it good?

I can answer this question by citing an instance. About twelve years ago, a newly organized banking-house, anxious for business, purchased, after what it believed to be sufficient investigation, an issue of bonds secured by a mortgage on a city street-railway. They had employed in the investigation a well known accountant, a man who at that time enjoyed a national reputation because of sensational disclosures of railway mismanagement. The accountant did not conduct the investigation personally. He sent his son in his stead, but he signed the report of earnings and expenses on the basis of which the banking-house purchased and sold the bonds.

RELIABLE INVESTMENT-BANKER

Shortly afterward, default in interest occurred. The bankers were astonished. They investigated. They found that their representative had been misled. He had accepted figures of earnings which were grossly exaggerated. The management, in order to make the necessary showing of earnings, had sold large quantities of tickets at wholesale rates, which the company had to redeem in transportation. These ticket-sales were counted as earnings. Expert accountant *fils* accepted the figures, which included these advance sales, as accurate representations of the financial condition of the company. Expert accountant *père* signed his son's report. The bankers had been grossly deceived by their incompetent representative. The company could not pay its interest. Its bonds were in default. Many of these bonds had been sold. What was to be done?

The bankers recognized that they were to blame. The investigation had been faulty. They had failed in their duty. They must take the consequences. They immediately offered to repurchase all bonds of this issue at the price paid. They actually did repurchase more than $300,000 of them, and carried them for seven years before they were able to recover the loss.

THE CAREFUL INVESTOR

Their case illustrates the nature as well as the limitations of the banker's responsibility. He must not misstate the facts about an investment to his clients. On the basis of these facts, he recommends the purchase of bonds as safe investments. If, however, the true state of affairs is not known to the banker; if, in ignorance of facts, a knowledge of which would make him refuse the purchase, he buys bonds and sells these to his customers, he is then morally bound to protect his customers against loss. A reputable banker will not shirk this obligation. He will not announce in his circulars that he will make good his customers' losses. He will not authorize his salesmen to make this statement. He will not formally admit his responsibility. But when the loss occurs, if it is his fault, or the fault of his agents who have not placed the true facts of the proposition before him, he will protect his customers.

Such cases are rare. I knew of one banking-house which had been in business for thirteen years, and which had had only two defaults among hundreds of issues which it has placed with investors. In only one case was the house responsible because of faulty investigation. In both cases its customers were protected. Another house has had three defaults in the same number of years, both due to technical and temporary causes. In each case the customers were protected.

Sometimes the banking-house will not go so far as to buy back defaulted bonds. If the company is sound, and the embarrassment certain to be temporary, the banker must take another course to protect his customers. A prominent banking-house of high reputation sold a large issue of bonds secured by a mortgage on the property of a public-service corporation. The bonds were perfectly secured, assuming that the management was honest. The stock-holding control of this company, however, thought to play a sharp trick on the bond-holders. They diverted earnings from interest into improvements, defaulted on the bonds, and secured the appointment of a receiver, thinking to force a compromise with the bond-holders.

The banking-house which had placed the bonds immediately took charge. They laid the true state of affairs before the bond-holders. They assured them that their investment was perfectly safe. They invited their coöperation in wresting the control from the dishonest management. Most of the bond-holders placed their interests in the hands of the banking-house which took charge of the reorganization, securing for the bond-holders in the new company not only the same interest which they had in the old company, but securities representing a large share of the profits in addition. This house has lost nothing of its high reputation by the course of action which it pursued in this matter.

I have said that the reputable investment-banker will always protect his clients. Yet how is the investor to distinguish between the reputable investment-bankers and those who look on bonds as the peddler regarded razors, as primarily made, not for service, but for sale. We can find plenty of bankers who will not protect their customers, who use them like a flock of sheep, shearing them from time to time, and yet, by some strange credulity which infests the minds of a certain type of investors, keeping their hold upon them.

I am familiar with the history of one of these firms. Strangely enough, its reputation is high in its city and State. Its members are counted among the prominent financiers of their community. Its list of clients is long and loyal. This firm has sold a number of issues of bonds whose security was bad and which have been in default. The head of the firm is quite frank about the matter. He once said that his customers did not mind bankruptcy. They were willing to go through reorganization. Some day they would make some money. A member of this firm expressed mild surprise at the painstaking investigation which another house thought it necessary to make before buying some bonds. He was asked how his house proceeded. "Well," he replied, "I guess we buy bonds by instinct." The record of his firm bears out his statement.

There is only one sure test of the character of a banking-house—its record of flotations. If we could have for every investment-banker who offers his wares to the public, a list of the bonds and stocks which he has offered for sale, the representations made at the time of issue, and the subsequent history of these securities, we should have a nearly infallible guide to his trustworthiness. Such a compilation could be easily made. It would, however, furnish a series of comparative revelations as to the records of various banking-houses, which would not only be illuminating but amazing. On the basis of such a record, the investor could place his money in full confidence that

the houses from whom he purchased were worthy
of his trust. I suggest to every investor that,
before buying any securities, he investigate the
record of the house which offers them. In most
cases he will find that record both fair and honorable. Such an investigation, however, may save
him from loss.

VII

PUBLIC OBLIGATIONS—MUNICIPAL BONDS PREFERRED

For the conservative investor who looks for absolute safety of principal, and who is willing to make some sacrifices of income in order to secure absolute safety, the municipal bond has the first choice. United States Government bonds, it is true, are safer, but the demands for these bonds from national banks, who use them as a basis for circulating notes, and to secure deposits of money with them by the government, is so great that they yield little more than 2 per cent. This yield is too small to be attractive even to the most conservative investor. Of the government bonds outstanding amounting to $963,349,390, $193,526,090 are held by national banks.

State bonds are distinctly inferior to municipal bonds. In the eleventh amendment to the Constitution of the United States it is provided that "the judicial power of the United States shall not be construed to extend to any suit in law or equity commenced or prosecuted against any of the

United States by citizens of another State, or by citizens or subjects of any foreign state." Under this amendment, any State may repudiate its obligations, and a number of States have done so, at different times, and for a variety of reasons. Following the panic of 1837, during a period of severe industrial depression, Pennsylvania, Maryland, Indiana, Illinois, Michigan, Florida, and Mississippi repudiated their debts, declared, in effect, that they were unable to pay their creditors. Of the four Northern States, Michigan was the only one which did not eventually pay in full. In the South, Florida and Mississippi were guilty of deliberate repudiation. Minnesota, in 1860, repudiated certain bonds issued in aid of railroad construction. These bonds were eventually redeemed at fifty cents on the dollar, with accrued interest. Following the Civil War, came a wave of repudiation in the South. From 1870 to 1884, nine Southern States defrauded their creditors by stopping payment on the bonds. A large part of this debt was due to the extravagance and rascality of the "carpet-bag" period, and these abuses were urged in defense and extenuation of the wholesale repudiation of written obligations. Whatever the cause, by 1870 the bonds of the Southern States in default had reached $170,025,340, an increase of $82,257,650 over the amount of defaulted debt in 1860.

There is a kindly and classical explanation of the tendency of the Southern States to repudiate, which applies, however, mainly to antebellum defaults. Mr. Justice Curtice, in an article in the *North American Review* for January, 1844, referring to a repudiation of debt by the State of Mississippi, says:

> To pay debts punctually is the point of honor among commercial peoples. But the planters of Mississippi do not so esteem it. They do not feel the importance of an exact conformity to contracts. It has not been their habit to meet the engagements on the very day, if not quite convenient. Certainly they attach no idea of dishonesty to such a course of dealing. They mean to pay, but they did not expect when they contracted the debt to distress themselves about the payment. If a friend wants a thousand dollars for a loan or a gift, he can have it, though perhaps a creditor wants it also. We do not mean to intimate that there are no high qualities in such a character, but they are different from those which make good bankers or merchants, and, therefore, bankers and merchants ought not to expect such men to look at a debt just as they do.

To explain the repudiation of the carpet-bag debts, we can resort to an illustration in another field. One of the favorite methods of swindling the farmer twenty years ago was by securing his signature to a document, one-half of which was a receipt, or bill of sale, or some such innocent thing, and the other half, which was folded under so as to be concealed from the victim's gaze, was a promise to pay. The innocuous part of the document would subsequently be cut off, and the promissory note, signed in ignorance of its real nature, and by the victim of a gross and palpable fraud, would be discounted at a bank. In time, this note would be presented for payment by the bank, an innocent holder for value, and entitled to collect on the fraudulent note.

In order to comprehend the attitude of the people of North Carolina or Mississippi toward their bonds issued during the reconstruction period we have only to picture the attitude of mind of the aforesaid farmer, supposing there was no law protecting the innocent holder for value of a negotiable instrument, when the bank which had purchased one of these fraudulent, though in form genuine, notes, asked for payment. Would he pay such a note? We think he would not. He would not even extend to the banker his sympathy. He would laugh in derision at the banker's calamity.

Now, this is exactly the attitude of the Southern States. There is no law which compels them to pay their debts. The construction of the United

States makes them immune from prosecution. No one can touch them. These debts, they claim, are tainted with fraud. They will not pay them, and look the whole world in the face when they say it.

There will come a time when these debts will be paid. These Southern States will need money for public improvements. In order to sell new bonds, they must first settle with existing creditors. This will not be a matter of sentiment or honor, but of business. When that time comes State bonds will improve their standing. At present, however, although some States, such as New York, enjoy excellent credit, the reputation of State bonds as a class is somewhat frowned upon.

Municipal bonds stand upon a different footing. Instead of the optional honesty of the State, an honesty depending on the prevalence and pre-dominance of the commercial spirit among her citizens, and upon the necessity of appealing from time to time for new loans to the creditors, we find in the municipal bond the guaranty of a secured obligation. Even in those States which have repudiated their written obligations, these smaller political units, the municipalities, enjoy excellent credit. Their bonds are in good demand, because both principal and interest are secured.

The explanation of this difference is found in the fact that these smaller governmental bodies do not enjoy the same immunity as the State. They can be sued by the creditor.

We hear much about the good faith of the public. We are told that it represents the distilled essence of a multitude of private consciences, that it is a higher, nobler, more dependable thing than the good faith of the individual. This view of public honor is not entirely correct. Edmund Burke, in his "Reflections on the Revolution in France," speaks of a perfect democracy as "the most shameless thing in the world." As he says:

> The share of infamy that is likely to fall to the lot of each individual in public acts is small indeed, the operation of opinion being in the inverse ratio to the number of those who abuse power. Their own approbation of their own acts has to them the appearance of a public judgment in their favor.

And in another place:

> Society requires not only that the passions of individuals should be subjected, but that even in the mass and body, as well as in the individual, the inclinations of men should frequently be thwarted, their will controlled, and their passions brought into subjection. This can only be done by a power out of themselves, and not, in the exercise of its function, subject to that will and to these passions which it is its office to bridle and subdue.

The State may be taken as the perfect democracy to which Burke refers. Some American

States are shameless, though populous with men honorable in all private business relations. The towns and cities of these States, however, are corporations, chartered by the State for the performance of the local functions of government, authorized to borrow money, and compelled by the law to repay what they have borrowed, by a "power outside of themselves."

The security of a municipal bond is twofold: first, the property not used for the purpose of government which the city may own, and which can be sold under execution in satisfaction of a judgment; and, second, the obligation of the municipal officers, when ordered to do so by the court, to levy taxes for the payment of principal and interest of their debts.

Some States provide in their constitutions that when a debt is incurred, provision must be made by taxation to repay the debt at maturity, and, in the meantime, to pay the interest. It is a general rule also, even when the constitution does not provide for such a tax, and also to supplement the constitutional requirement, that the local authorities should, by municipal ordinance, provide for the tax. Even without special provisions in State constitution or local ordinance, the general power of taxation can be invoked by the creditor in case of default, and court orders can compel public officers to levy the tax.

Municipal bonds differ from the bonds of private corporations in that they must be issued in strict compliance with the law. The history of municipal borrowing in the United States abounds with instances of folly. Bonds have been issued in aid of public improvements which never materialized. Bonds have been sold to enormous amounts whose proceeds never found their way into the public treasury. Every financial wrong inflicted on the Southern people by the reconstruction governments can find its counterpart in the borrowing by Northern municipalities. Learning wisdom by experience, the people have, in their State constitutions, and in the statutes under which municipal corporations are chartered, imposed upon those bodies a variety of restrictions. These restrictions, since they enforce caution and conservatism upon the municipal authorities, contribute also to the security of the investor.

In the first place, municipalities are generally prohibited from incurring debt in aid of any railroad or other outside enterprise. The proceeds of municipal bond sales must be spent in and for the benefit of the borrowing community.

The amount of the debt is closely limited. The standard of limitation is the assessed value of the property in the town or city. With few exceptions, the assessed value is far below, usually little more than half, the market value. On the basis of this assessed value, cities are prohibited from incurring more than small percentages, ranging from 1½ to 15 per cent. of debt. A limit of five per cent. on the assessed valuation, a common restriction, with an assessment of 50 per cent. of selling value, is equivalent to a stipulation that the city must not borrow more than 2½ per cent. of the amount at which its taxable property should be valued.

The State also takes great care that loans should be incurred only after full deliberation by the municipal authorities; in many States, after the voters have had an opportunity to pass upon the wisdom of the loan. The utmost care is taken to secure complete publicity. In order that the highest price shall be obtained, competitive bids are invited, accompanied by certified checks for substantial amounts as evidence of good faith. In every possible way, the State protects the public, and, in so doing, protects the investor against excessive bond issues, for purposes of which the people do not approve, or for which the issuing municipalities do not receive full value.

These legal restrictions on municipal borrowing while they protect the investor when observed, also make it necessary for him to be on his guard to see that they have been fully complied with. When a railroad company issues bonds, every provision of its charter and by-laws may have been violated by the making of the loan, and yet the innocent holder of these bonds will be protected. He is not supposed to have knowledge of or to be held responsible for the internal arrangements of the company to which he loans money. He has done his part by giving value for the bonds. If the company has been defrauded of a part of the proceeds of these bonds, or if they have been issued for a purpose which the charter forbids, the company should look for compensation and reimbursement to those officials who are responsible.

With a municipal bond, the case is different. The regulations which govern their issue are a part of the laws of their State. Every one is supposed to have knowledge of them. The bond-buyer must have these regulations in mind. He must assume that they have been complied with. If, in any substantial respect, these regulations have not been closely followed, the bonds may be held invalid. A little book entitled "Municipal Bonds Held Void," by Maurice B. Dean, of the New York Bar, gives a complete list of those obligations in the purchase of which the creditor lost. From this digest I take the following:

In 1904, $4,000 of bonds issued by the village of Grant, Nebraska, were held invalid "because they were issued in aid of private water-works," an unlawful purpose. As authority for their issue, the bonds referred to a statute which did not convey authority. The court said: "The bonds, therefore, bear upon their face ample evidence of their own invalidity, and no one can claim to be a bona fide purchaser of a bond which carried on its face evidence of its unlawful character."

A Michigan case is even more significant. The village of Ashley sold $8,500 of water-works bonds under a resolution of the village council, which, while it authorized the president and clerk to sign water-works bonds, did not authorize the president to deliver the bonds. The bonds, having been 'delivered without authority, were held to be void, although in the hands of a bona fide holder."

An Indiana case shows how far the taint of illegality can persist. The city of Jeffersonville had issued and sold bonds to obtain money to contest litigation changing the county seat. At a later time it desired to take up these bonds with a new issue. The issue was enjoined by a tax-payer, and the original issue was held to be void because made for an illegal purpose."

Out of this situation arises the need of a careful legal investigation before municipal bonds can be safely offered to the investor. The buyer of a municipal bond cannot be an innocent holder for value. Ignorance of the law cannot be urged in his favor. He is charged with constructive knowledge of any illegality in the procedure under which his bonds were issued. If every requirement laid down in the law to govern the issue of the bonds has not been complied with, his bonds are invalid.

This does not mean that the bond-holder will necessarily lose. He can still fall back on the good faith of the people, estimating this at its problematical value. But the trouble is that after bonds have been tainted with illegality, there is no legal way in which they can be paid, except by popular subscription, until the law is changed. The city of Helena, Montana, through no fault of its own, is unable to pay certain bonds which, owing to a decline in the value of the city's property, are issued to an illegal amount. The city stands ready to pay these bonds whenever a legal method can be found. Meanwhile the holders suffer loss.

The bond-house purchasing an issue of municipals, therefore, centres its inquiry upon the legality of the issue. It takes into account other factors— the productiveness of the assets, such as waterworks, which are to be constructed with the proceeds of the bonds; the population of the borrowing community, its record of good faith toward its creditors, the assessed value of the property, and any other factors which may bear upon the merits of the flotation as a business proposition.

The chief concern of the banking house is with the legality of the municipal bond issue. Municipal, school district, and county bonds are good, if they are legal. The margin of a security in the value of a town's property over the total amount which it is allowed to borrow is so great as to eliminate the element of business risk which the purchaser of railroad bonds, for example, must consider. The bond-house, for this investigation, relies upon the advice of the best lawyers it can secure. In some cases the opinions of two firms are taken.

The lawyer's statement to the bond-house answers the following questions:

(1) Is the city permitted by its charter and by the State constitution and Acts of Assembly to issue bonds for the purposes proposed?

(2) Have the necessary formalities, such as passage of ordinances, approval by the mayor, etc., been taken by the city?

(3) If necessary, has the bond issue been approved at an election, and in that case, has the election been conducted according to the prescribed form?

(4) Have the legal stipulations concerning advertisement, secrecy of bids, and award to the highest bidder been complied with?

(5) Is the amount of the issue within the limits set by the statute?

(6) Is the form of the bond such that the city cannot escape responsibility by any technicality or slip in drawing up or wording the instrument?

(7) Have the present bonds, or the bonds which it is proposed to refund with this issue, ever been subject to litigation?

On the basis of these legal opinions, for which the bond-house must sometimes pay large fees, the bonds are offered to the investor, who may purchase them with absolute confidence in their validity. Mr. Lawrence Chamberlain, in his excellent work "The Principles of Bond Investment," states that in 1907, out of $200,000,000 of municipal and State bonds issued, some $4,000,000, of 2 per cent., divided among 65 municipal issues, were finally declined by those who had bought them subject to the approval of their attorneys, usually on the ground of their illegality.

To show the care exercised in this matter, I recall an instance where a New York house refused to purchase an issue of school-district bonds, because, while the law required that the notice of the election to authorize the bonds should be posted for a certain time on the *front* door of the school-house, it appeared that the notice had been posted on the *side* door.

In some States—New Jersey, North Dakota, Texas, Georgia and Kansas—the law now provides for a "State certificate of validity" usually endorsed on the bond by some State official. When this safeguard is provided, a legal investigation is not absolutely necessary, although it will usually be made as an extra precaution. Elsewhere, however, the investigation by the attorneys is indispensable to security.

VIII

HIGH-YIELD MUNICIPAL BONDS

It is not going too far to say that the bonds of American cities rank among the safest investments in the world. We find, however, that outside of institutions, especially savings-banks and the more conservative class of investors, municipal bonds are not popular. The reason is that in the section of the country where most of the funds available for investment are concentrated—the Northern States—the bonds of municipalities sell at much higher figures, thus offering little inducement to the investor. In the State of New York, for example, we find the prevailing yield on municipal bonds to be from 4 to 4.20 per cent. In New Jersey the rate sometimes runs higher, although some of the bonds of Newark, at the last quotation, yielded no more than 3.95 per cent. to the investor. In the New England States, the yield on municipal bonds is very small. The bonds of Boston yield only 3.90 per cent. and the bonds of Connecticut, whose quotations are available, show from 4.05 to 4.10 per cent. When we pass outside the North-eastern States we find an immediate, although only a moderate, advance in the yield on bonds. Bonds of Michigan range from a minimum of 4.50 per cent. to a maximum of 4.60 per cent.; the municipal bonds of South Dakota run from 4.30 to 4.65 per cent. In Tennessee the range is about the same. In Texas some good municipal bonds can be purchased to yield 5 per cent.

The difference between the yields of the municipal bonds in the East, and in the West and South, is due to the concurrence of several influences. The investment funds are largely concentrated in the East. There is a prejudice in the minds of all investors in favor of the bonds of their own localities. This prejudice is also enacted into law in the restrictions placed upon the investments of savings-banks. These banks are the principal buyers of municipal bonds, and the immense demands of these institutions are concentrated upon a limited number of issues. For example, the savings-bank law of Massachusetts limits the investment of savings funds to the bonds or notes of any city of the five New England States, or of any county, town, or water district, which conforms to certain restrictions as to the relation between indebtedness and valuation.

Outside of New England, Massachusetts savings-banks can buy municipal bonds of New York, Ohio, Pennsylvania, Indiana, Illinois, Michigan, Wisconsin, Minnesota, Missouri, Iowa, and the District of Columbia, when issued by a city of more than 30,000 inhabitants, and where the net debt does not exceed 5 per cent. of the assessed valuation.

Similar restrictions are found in all the States, and these restrictions have the effect of so concentrating the demand for municipal bonds as to make a marked difference in their price. An issue by a small town in Massachusetts, for example, may be no better, nor even as good, as the bonds of Oklahoma City. The Oklahoma City bonds, however, will sell on a 4⅞ per cent. basis, while the bonds of Pittsfield, Massachusetts, will sell on a 3⅝ per cent. basis. There is no question about the honesty of the people of Oklahoma City, or of the value of their property, or of the industrial future of their city. The bonds of Oklahoma City are perfectly good. They are not, however, available for a certain restricted class of investment, and there is a natural prejudice against them on the part of Eastern investors. This explains their low price and high yield.

HIGH-YIELD MUNICIPAL BONDS

There is another class of municipal bonds issued by tax districts, which, when issued under proper restrictions, and purchased from reliable bond-houses, give the investor excellent security and high return. I have before me the 6 per cent. bonds of a certain levee district in one of the Southern States. The valuation of taxable property in this district is $1,250,000, and the total debt is $160,000. The present value of the land in the district is from $15 to $40 per acre. The issuing bond-houses state that land outside the district, which is not subject to flooding, sells from $75 to $100 per acre. The total area of the district is 59,596 acres, and the debt, per acre, is only $2.68, or less than 20 per cent. of the value of the cheapest land in the district.

Another illustration of tax-district bonds comes from Seattle in an issue of $30,000 ten-year 6 per cent. bonds, issued for regrading certain streets adjacent to the main business centre of Seattle. A large number of offerings of this kind are available to the investor.

In view of these high interest rates, usually ranging from 5 to 6 per cent. or higher, and also because of the lack of familiarity of the Eastern investor with such issues, it is important to understand the security back of these bonds. All tax districts, such as school districts, levee districts, irrigation districts, or sewerage districts, are agencies of the State which have been established to serve local public purposes. These districts sometimes coincide with the areas of municipalities, and sometimes include parts of several municipalities. The issuing of the obligations for the financing of a local improvement of this character is usually authorized at a special election. At this election, a stated majority of the voters living in a certain locality which is to be benefited by particular improvements, such, for instance, as the regrading of certain streets in Seattle, or the construction of a levee in Louisiana, must signify their willingness to pay special taxes which are to be levied on the property benefited.

The improvement will increase the value of the property. The owners of the property are willing to pay the cost of the improvement, and the fund to pay the cost will be created by the improvement which, if wisely planned and properly made, should increase the value of the property far more than the amount of the incumbrance placed upon it by the bond issue. These special tax-district bonds are considered apart from the municipal debts of the town, a part or all of whose area may be included in the tax district. The burden is borne, not by all the tax-payers, but by a particular group of tax-payers.

The usual remedy provided in case of default on special assessment bonds is the same as that provided for the collection of municipal bonds proper. For example, in Kansas, the holder of improvement bonds, for which the law provides special assessments against adjacent property, is entitled to mandamus, ordering a general tax levy to pay his judgment, and the city can then reimburse itself by levying assessments upon the property affected.

Special assessment bonds are sometimes given special security. In Illinois, for example, bridge districts issue bonds which are a direct lien on the property of the district. On the bond, before it can be negotiated, the owner of each piece of property must place this endorsement, and his agreement that the property shall become liable for the interest and principal of the obligation, and that the bonds shall be a lien upon the property until it is paid off and discharged.

The issue of tax-district bonds is a method of evading the law which limits the borrowing power of municipalities. It is equally certain, however, that in view of the conservatism of American legislative bodies on the subject of municipal debts, the special dispensations given to districts who borrow money for public improvements are not likely to be abused. In nearly all cases, these special assessment bonds are sold to obtain money for public improvements which will greatly increase the value of the property affected. A final argument in their favor is that this property is specifically liable for the repayment of the bonds. We may conclude, therefore, that in the bonds of tax districts there is offered to the investor an obligation which combines the advantages of high yield and good security, security which is, on the whole, better than can be furnished him by most private corporations. With the continued development of the newer sections of the United States, these tax-district bonds will come upon the market in increasing volume. A study of the advantages which they offer will repay the investor who wishes to combine security and high return.

IX

THE AMERICAN RAILWAY INDUSTRY

GREATEST of all sources of investment is the American Railway. For forty years the transportation companies of the United States have poured into the world's investment-market a flood of securities. The savings of Europe and America have found their largest single outlet in railway stocks and bonds. The volume of railway securities now outstanding presents a vast total. Of railway stocks there were outstanding at the close of 1911, $8,582,000,000; of railway bonds, $10,091,000,000. This sum is more than twice the national debts of the entire civilized world. It is the largest single contribution to the world's savings. If we except the value of land, it exceeds, in size and value, all other forms of investment in the United States combined.

Of recent years, railway investments have declined in favor. Other bonds and stocks have entered the competition. Public hostility has been aroused against the railways. They have been subjected to severe regulation, denied the right to advance their rates, in many cases forced to reduce them. Long enjoying a monopoly of the investment market, railway directors have hesitated to meet the demand for high-interest bonds. They have halted and hesitated, postponing the inevitable surrender to the demand for securities paying more than four per cent.

We have here an explanation of the decreasing output of railway securities in recent years, and this, in turn, explains the slow progress of railway construction during the same period. Observe the figures. From 1880 to 1890 our railway mileage increased from 93,262 to 166,703; from 1890 to 1900, although this was a period of panic and depression, drought and scanty harvests, the growth in mileage was 166,703 to 194,262. From 1900 to 1910, however, a period of enormous growth in other lines of business, the railway system increased 48,845 miles. In 1911 only 3,465 miles were constructed.

This small growth in mileage does not mean that American railroads are standing still. During the last decade they have spent, measured by the increase in their liabilities, $6,719,000,000 upon the properties. The expenditure has, however, been rather devoted to improving facilities than to building new lines. Immense tunnels, the Pennsylvania and New York Central in New York, the North-western in Chicago; costly projects of electrification, such as that carried through by the New Haven and Hartford; replacement of wooden by steel equipment, and large additions to equipment, have engaged the capital available for railroad construction.

In five years, from 1903 to 1907, 14,424 locomotives and 536,942 freight and passenger cars were put into service. Each year's additions, moreover, are of larger locomotives, and cars of greater cost and capacity. Vast sums have also been spent on the purchase of costly city real estate required for larger terminal yards. Track elevation, installation of block-signals, reduction of grades, and elimination of curves, have all taken substantial shares of railway funds.

The American railway industry, considering its size, and the large number of companies operating it, is the soundest and strongest business in the world. Observe, first, the size of the plant and personnel: mileage, 359,000; cars, 2,408,589; locomotives, 65,310; employees, 1,699,420. Over 10,000,000 Americans draw their living from the railroads.

The business which is conducted by this great organization is worthy of it. In 1912 American railroads transported 1,817,562,049 tons of freight and 1,019,658,605 passengers. Expressed on a mileage basis, these figures are even more striking. Over every mile of American railroad in 1910 were carried 1,071,086 tons of freight and 138,169 passengers. This immense business was done, moreover, at a very moderate cost to the shipper and passenger, a fact proven by an average freight rate of .748 cents per ton per mile and a passenger rate of 2.22 cents per passenger per mile. No other industry, moreover, performs its service or furnishes its goods at so small a margin of profit. In the opinion of the best informed railway men, the passenger business is operated without profit; and out of the three-fourths of a cent received for each ton carried one mile, it is a safe estimate that not more than one-fourth of a cent represents profit.

In spite of these small profits on each unit of business handled, the railway industry is highly profitable, owing to the great volume of the traffic. For the year ending December 31, 1911, the total profits of 246,655 miles of railroad operated were $1,085,951,595, or, deducting taxes, $972,237,934. The railway industry, on a gross business of about three billion dollars ($2,848,468,965), makes a profit of nearly one billion dollars. A business which can show one dollar in three as profit over the cost of operation is properly characterized as the most profitable business in the United States. Even the United States Steel Corporation, generally recognized as the most profitable of the large industrials, now that the Standard Oil and American Tobacco Companies have been dissolved, in its best year, 1907, on a gross business of $757,-014,767.68 showed $177,201,561 of profits.

And this introduces us to the second characteristic of the railway industry which especially recommends railway securities to the investor. Not only is the railway business profitable, but its prosperity is continuous, and its profits are, therefore, subject to smaller fluctuations. In 1908, the year following one of the severest panics in our history, railway profits declined only 6.2 per cent., and in 1909 they more than regained the loss. In good times and in bad, railway profits not only hold their own, but tend strongly to advance.

The reason for this movement of profits it is important to understand. Profits of a business depend primarily upon the demand for its products. If that demand is sporadic and intermittent, the business will be, as Andrew Carnegie said of steel, either "a prince or a pauper." But if the demand is continuous, fluctuating within narrow limits, always tending upward, and if the business shows a large margin over cost of operation, we have, from the investor's standpoint, an ideal situation. Such a condition prevails in the railway world.

The advantage of the railway industry from the standpoint of stability of profits is well illustrated by a comparison of the gross earnings of the Pennsylvania Railroad with those of the United States Steel Corporation. The one is the largest railroad system of the United States and one of the best managed, and the other is the largest and one of the best managed and best organized industries. The steel corporation, moreover, manufactures a great variety of products, so that its demand would naturally be more stable than those of steel manufacturing companies whose profits are more narrowly specialized. It has also been able to maintain, for long periods, stable prices for most of its products, and its supremacy in the steel trade since its organization has only recently been challenged. Competition, until the winter of 1909, very slightly disturbed it, and yet the fluctuation of its gross earnings, compared with the Pennsylvania Railroad, which appears in the following table, where the figures are stated in millions of dollars, is extreme. The figures for the

Pennsylvania Railroad are as follows, stated in millions of dollars:

1902.. 112
1903.. 122
1904.. 118
1905.. 133
1906.. 148
1907.. 164
1908.. 136

and for the United States Steel Corporation as follows:

1902.. 500
1903.. 536
1904.. 444
1905.. 585
1906.. 696
1907.. 757
1908.. 482

The percentages of fluctuations from one year to another in the two companies are as follows:

	Pennsylvania Railroad	U.S. Steel Corporation.
1902..............................	15.15	.....
1903..............................	+8.93	+7.20
1904..............................	−3.28	−17.16
1905	+12.71	+31.76
1906..............................	+11.28	+18.97
1907..............................	+10.81	+8.76
1908..............................	−17.08	−36.33

Broadly speaking, the distinction which has been indicated between railway and manufacturing industries holds good wherever it is applied. The demand for transportation services offered by some railways, especially those which depend exclusively upon iron and steel or kindred industries, is more irregular than those of some manufacturing companies—for example, gas or electric lighting companies or companies supplying certain food products which are regarded as necessaries of life. But as between the two classes of corporations, railroads and industrials, the railway has a marked advantage in the greater stability of the demand for its service.

The railway industry is also distinguished by its comparative freedom from competition. What manufacturing industry has vainly tried to accomplish by unlawful combination, the railroads have achieved without conscious effort, solely by virtue of their economic position. The cost of duplicating their plant is so great as to protect them in the enjoyment of the traffic of which they have gained control.

From every standpoint, the investor is correct in the marked preference which he has always shown in favor of railway securities. We turn next to consider certain weaknesses in the railroad's position which arise out of its position as a public servant.

X

RAILWAY LABOR AND RAILWAY INVESTMENT

THE most important problem before the American people is the problem of railway development. America is still an undeveloped country. Three-fourths of the United States, industrially considered, lies north of the Ohio and east of the Mississippi River. The West and South are yet in the infancy of their business development.

The realization of the immense possibilities of this country must depend upon the extension and development of our railroad facilities. It has been estimated by men whose opinions carry great weight, that at least one billion dollars each year for many years to come should be spent in railroad building and rebuilding. Some of this new construction will be immediately profitable. On the largest part, the profits will be deferred. That vast expenditure which is demanded by consideration of public safety and convenience may never be profitable.

In recent years, railway construction has lagged

behind the progress of other industries. A present indication of this fact is the impending shortage of railway equipment. A business revival has just begun, and already the inadequacy of the transportation system to carry the expected increase in traffic is conceded.

The railroads are unprepared, not because they have not foreseen the return of good times, but because of certain factors in the situation which make directors hesitate to invest great sums of money, even when the condition of their credit permits great sums of money to be raised.

This feeling of doubt and distrust of the future, which is everywhere encountered among railway officials and financiers, is due, first, to the apparent determination of the Interstate Commerce Commission not to allow any general advance in rates, and, second, to the increasing pressure of the Railway Brotherhoods for higher wages.

If railway expenses are not increased, the present scale of rates will yield satisfactory profits. But, from the attitude of railway labor, railway expenses will increase. The announced determination of the railway labor organizations to increase the wages of their members is, from the standpoint of the railway and of the country, of far more serious import than the unyielding attitude of the Commerce Commission.

It is a trite saying but a true one, that transportation is the life-blood of commerce. The specialization of different regions to those industries in which, from the character of the population, their natural resources, or their proximity to markets, they have peculiar advantages has been carried so far in this country that free and continuous interchange of commodities is indispensable, not only to industry, but to existence. Suspend the operation of the railroads of the United States for one week, and the resulting damage would be almost incalculable. It would be measured not in money and in goods alone, but in human suffering and human life. How many cities in this country are provisioned for one week? How long would the supply of fuel and material for the mills and factories suffice, if fresh supplies were interrupted? The answers to these questions are furnished by every snow-storm which ties up the railroads of a section even for a few days. Every business in the region feels the effect. The whole population suffers inconvenience, and the business losses are heavy.

How much more serious would be the effect of

a general and a protracted suspension of railroad transportation. It would be a national calamity comparable to the effects of war or pestilence, a catastrophe which it is almost unthinkable that any body of men, for their own ends, however worthy and reasonable those ends might be, would combine to bring upon the country; or, to look at the matter from another standpoint, it is even more unthinkable that the responsible heads of the railway companies would allow a general suspension of railway operation to take place if the most extreme concession on their part could prevent.

Into this situation of absolute dependence upon the continuous operation of the railroads, a situation fraught with the possibilities of national disaster, enter the Brotherhoods with their periodical demands for increases in wages, reduction in hours, and more favorable conditions of employment.

One set of these demands made by the Brotherhood of Trainmen is now being considered by the Trunk Lines. The Firemen and Engineers have recently gained important concessions from arbitration boards. As soon as this difficulty is settled, and from past experience a portion at least of the demands of the union will be granted, the never-ending controversy will be transferred to some other section or some other organization. The pressure of the unions upon the railroads is increasing and unceasing.

In these discussions and contests, organized railway labor possesses a predominant advantage. They know just how valuable their services are. They know that the trains must run, and that no men outside their organizations can run them. Consider for a moment the extent of their advantage by comparison with labor contests in other fields. If the anthracite miners strike, the country suffers, but there are ways of escape for the consumer. We can turn to bituminous coal or gas, and there are reserves of anthracite to draw upon. If the bituminous miners strike, the users of bituminous coal can live for a time on their own reserves, or they can change their grates to burn anthracite. The last great strike in the iron and steel industry had little more than a local significance and effect.

Let the railroad men strike, however, and, as 1877 and 1894 showed, the entire country feels the blow. Every class, every community, every business, is affected. The four Railway Brotherhoods hold in their hands the prosperity of the United States. Because they possess a monopoly of the skilled labor necessary to conduct the business of transportation, they have the power to cripple every business in the country. Skilled railway operators cannot be replaced by non-union men. For locomotive engineers or firemen there are few substitutes. If they cease to labor, the trains cease to move, commerce comes to a standstill, factories close, business staggers and stops. The effect of the suspension of cash payments by the banks in 1907 is still remembered. The situation at that time gave but a faint indication of the damage which the country would sustain by the suspension of the railroads.

Railway managers know this. Railway employees know this. In every controversy over wages, hours of employment, or working conditions, the unique position of the railway, as an indispensable public servant, and the extraordinarily powerful position of the employee of that public servant, are present in the minds of the contestants. Such a contest is unequal. The men have all the advantage. They can throw the railroads into bankruptcy and the country into ruin, and they know it. They know further that the railway managers will not be allowed by public opinion, even if their own dispositions set in this direction, to force the issue. They must make concessions; they must, in every contest, yield something. All, therefore, that is required is for the men to return again, and yet again, with ever-increasing demands, and they can obtain the entire surplus revenue of the railroad.

I do not claim that the railway employees will carry their demands to this extent, or that the desire to confiscate the dividends of the railway stock-holders has ever entered the minds of their leaders. They have it in their power, however, to advance their wages to the point where the present scale of dividends can no longer be maintained. When Lord Clive, on his return from India, was accused in the House of Commons of the practice of extortion, he replied, "Sir, when I think what I might have taken, I am astonished at my own moderation." With equal justice, the Railway Brotherhoods can point to the evidence of their moderation in the fact that the railroads can still pay dividends and lay aside something for their surplus accounts.

This situation is, however, fraught with possibilities of peril. So far as the Interstate Commerce

Commission is concerned, the railroads have little to fear. If the Commission will not sanction a general advance in rates, it is unlikely that it will order their general reduction. Railway rates, the products of innumerable adjustments and compromises, tend constantly to stability. Each year the difficulty of change, because of the wider-reaching consequences of change, becomes greater. Adjustments between localities and classes of traffic, reductions in special cases, may be made; but the danger of a general reduction in rates which shall affect earnings is slight.

It is not so with the labor situation. Here the representatives of organized labor have set no limit to their demands, short of the utmost ability of the railroads to pay. Railway wages, in their opinion, will never be high enough. They are willing to endorse the railroads' demands for higher rates, out of which higher wages might be paid, and, in fact, this proposition has been seriously advanced by some of their leaders. They will not, however, concede that railway wages can be limited, that, for example, the locomotive engineer should be restricted to a maximum of $80 per month, a salary upon which he can purchase his house and send his children to the high school.

They desire that his wages should rise to $250 per month, upon which he can send his children to college. No matter how high railway wages go, they are still too low, in the opinion of the railway employee, for his necessities, his responsibilities and his deserts.

And, after all, if only these demands can be reconciled with the necessities of the country for a full development of its resources, and with the just claims of the railroad stock-holders and creditors, why should the railway employee be denied his wish to rise to a higher plane of existence? Every day millions of people trust their lives to the men who run the trains, walk the tracks, and operate the signals and switches. What compensation will be considered too much for the faithful performance of this trust? What public servant has a more responsible position than the locomotive engineer? Who has charge of a larger amount of property? Upon whose competence and vigilance depend so large a number of human lives?

Let us come to the issue of the question: How can the demands of the railway men be met; demands which they apparently have present power to enforce; however gradually, with whatever degree of conservatism they go about enforcing them; while at the same time the needs of the country for additional capital may be satisfied? Under present conditions, the profits of the railroads, present and prospective, large though they are, are not large enough to induce a sufficient amount of investment to meet the national requirements. The country has had abundant proof that in recent years sufficient money has not been spent upon railway facilities. Unless the outlook for railway profits becomes more favorable, these facilities will become increasingly inadequate.

What, then, is to be done? Shall rates be advanced to permit the payment of higher wages? How will this mend matters? If rates go up and wages rise with them, shippers and consumers are burdened and railway credit is not improved. It is by following no such vicious circle that the solution of the problem is to be found. The United States will never reach a permanent solution of its transportation problem until railway labor can be brought to realize and recognize by its acts that the railroads are entitled—in the words of the Supreme Court—"To a reasonable return upon a fair value of their property employed in the public service." This reasonable return is not to be the rate of interest on the best first mortgages; but such a rate of profit, averaging good years with bad, as will attract capital into railroad securities. More than this the railroad stockholder does not and should not claim; less than this means an arrested railway development, a slow and halting industrial development, a condition of prolonged business stagnation, broken only by. fitful gleams of temporary prosperity.

XI

"A REASONABLE RETURN UPON THE VALUE OF THE PROPERTY DEVOTED TO THE PUBLIC SERVICE"

In the words which form the title to this Chapter, Mr. Charles A. Prouty, speaking for the Interstate Commerce Commission, on February 22, 1911, stated the problem presented to the Commission by the petition of the Trunk Lines that they should be allowed to advance their rates. "We are to determine," said the Commission, "whether the net return of these carriers upon the value of their property devoted to the public service will be sufficient without an advance in their rates."

After an exhaustive review of the testimony presented on behalf of and against the railroads, the Commission reached the conclusion that these defendants have not established such a need for additional revenue as justifies, at this time, an increase in these rates. This decision was, however, without prejudice to the railroads.

It has been several times stated in the course of this discussion that in view of the complex character of this problem, nothing but an actual test can satisfactorily determine the financial results from the operations of these several carriers. There is no evidence before us which establishes the necessity for higher rates. The probability is that increased rates will not be necessary in the future. In view of the liberal returns received by these defendants in the past ten years, they should be required to show, with reasonable certainty, the necessity before the increase is allowed. If actual results should demonstrate that our forecast of the future is wrong, there might be ground for asking a further consideration of this subject.

The railroads have again petitioned to be allowed to make a five per cent. advance in all rates in Official Classification Territory, north of the Ohio and east of the Mississippi rivers, an advance equivalent to a $40,000,000 increase in net revenues. If their officials were not convinced that the "actual test" asked for by the Commission had demonstrated that the Commission was wrong, the railroads would not make attempt to increase their rates. What, then, is the nature of this experience of the last three years, upon which the railroads must rely if they are to induce the Commission to reconsider its decision of 1911?

This question must be answered with reference to the evidence and reasoning upon which the Commission's former refusal was based. In substance this was as follows: The Pennsylvania, Baltimore and Ohio, and New York Central are typical trunk-line railroads. Their freight revenues were nearly one-half of the total freight revenue in Official Classification Territory. "Whatever rate might reasonably be imposed upon these three systems must be held to be a reasonable charge for that service by all lines."

The Commission defined a reasonable return upon the property of these three companies to be a margin of profits equivalent to certain earnings upon their common stocks. For the Baltimore and Ohio, it was held that "the sum remaining after fixed charges, including as a fixed charge the dividend upon the preferred stock, should be equivalent to between 7 and 8 per cent. upon the common stock," or about $2,280,000—1½ per cent. on the present common stock. For the Pennsylvania, a margin of $18,000,000 over common-stock dividends was held not to be unreasonable. For the New York Central, the Commission found that, after allowing for an expected increase in operating expenses due to the higher wage scale which went into effect in 1910, the Company could pay its 6 per cent. dividends with about $1,500,000 to spare. For several reasons; an admitted inflation of the capital of the constituent companies and of the New York Central at the time of the consolidation in 1869, amounting to $57,000,000, on which stock issued without consideration to the company, $120,000,000 in dividends had been paid, and not omitting to mention the fact that the New York Central was burdened with unprofitable leases, losses on which the public should not be expected to make up to its stockholders in higher rates, and having regard, finally, to the exceptionally strong position of certain of the New York Central's subsidiaries, the Commission reached the conclusion that this margin of $1,500,000 over the dividend requirement was not so small as to warrant an increase of freight rates in order to increase it.

We have, then, this standard by which to determine the reasonableness of rates in Official Classification Territory. If it appears that existing rates now yield these three companies substantially less than the amount of profits which the Interstate Commerce Commission, in 1911, declared to be reasonable, then the carriers will have established their case. If, on the other hand, the dividends of these three typical companies, notwithstanding higher operating costs and increased fixed charges, are still protected by the same relative margins of safety as those which the Commission considered adequate in 1911, then the railroads have lost their case before they open it.

THE CAREFUL INVESTOR

The facts of railway profits for the last year for which statistics are available are as follows for each of the three companies under examination:

Pennsylvania Railroad Company—Year Ending December 31, 1912:

Net Income	$42,153,964
Dividends 6 per cent	27,198,918
Balance	$14,955,046

Baltimore and Ohio—Year Ending June 30, 1912:

Balance of Net Income or for Preferred Dividends	$11,543,000
Dividends on common 6 per cent	9,121,073
Balance	$ 2,421,927

New York Central and Hudson River Railroad—Year Ending December 31, 1912:

Balance of Net Income over all charges	$13,879,837
Dividends (5 per cent.)	11,136,465
Balance	$ 2,743,372
Amount required to pay 6 per cent., the standard accepted by the Commission in 1911	$13,563,558
Balance—over 6 per cent	316,279

Summarized, these results are as follows:

Balance of Net Earnings over charges accepted by the Commission as standard in 1911:

Baltimore and Ohio	$ 2,280,000
Pennsylvania	18,000,000
New York Central	1,500,000

Balance of Net Earnings over charges for last fiscal year:

Baltimore and Ohio	$ 2,421,927
Pennsylvania	14,955,918
New York Central	316,279

A REASONABLE RETURN

From these figures it appears that, measured by the standard accepted by the Interstate Commerce Commission, the Baltimore and Ohio is in about the same relative position as in 1910, the New York Central has suffered a severe decline in its margin of safety, and the margin of safety of the Pennsylvania has seriously decreased.

On the basis of the Commission's reasoning in 1911, and taking no account of changes in conditions affecting the railroads since that time, the carriers are evidently entitled to an increase in rates.

It is also possible to advance additional arguments in support of the railroad's contention, based on alleged changes in conditions affecting the railroads since 1910.

Operating expenses have rapidly increased, outstripping the substantial gains in gross earnings. For this the demands of organized labor are mainly responsible and these show no signs of abatement.

The investment situation is not satisfactory. Weak companies are continually facing financial difficulties. Some companies, hitherto reported strong, have been shown to be extremely weak. Many strong companies are turning from one emergency expedient to another in the attempt to finance their maturing obligations. Railroads must apparently pay five per cent. for money, and until the international financial situation clears, they may have difficulty in filling their requirements, even at that high figure.

Public regulation is, moreover, growing more exacting. Greater safety in travel, improved working conditions and shorter hours for employes, the provision of improved facilities for shippers, such regulations are becoming universal, and each one adds to the cost of railway operation. The railroads have suffered, in common with all industries, from the rising prices of their operating supplies, of which coal is the most important. Their costs of construction and repair have also greatly increased for the same reason.

On the other hand, it is possible to advance some considerations on behalf of the shippers and against the increase of rates. The method followed by the Interstate Commerce Commission takes account only of the profits of companies, disregarding the profits of groups of companies. Back of the New York Central, for example, is a group of wealthy and prosperous subsidiaries, which have earned far more than they have paid to the parent company in dividends. The same is true of the Pennsylvania. Again, the present stringency in the investment market is not permanent. Railway securities will improve in market and price, especially after the companies, as the Pennsylvania is now doing, have reorganized their capital accounts by creating general refunding mortgages under which bonds of a kind acceptable to investors can be sold.

It has not been shown that railway efficiency has reached the practicable maximum. Indeed recent investigations of the New Haven and Hartford show that efficiency can be largely increased.

Finally, it does not appear that the railroads would be allowed to retain the $40,000,000 which is the estimated amount of the yield from the increase in rates in Official Classification Territory. Railway labor is not yet satisfied, and assessments upon railway property are steadily advancing. The final result might be that the shipper has made a substantial contribution, not to the railroads, but to the railway employes and to the State.

Before the increase in rates is granted, the entire subject of the financial situation of the railroads will be carefully investigated by the Interstate Commerce Commission. It is to be hoped that the result of this investigation will be the formation of some conclusions and standards of permanent value in the determination of what constitutes a reasonable railway rate.

XII

THE SECURITIES OF PUBLIC-SERVICE
CORPORATIONS

THE public-service corporation is so-called because it supplies a service or a commodity to the entire population of a community. As an aid to the performance of this public service, it is allowed to occupy the public streets and other public property with pipes, wires, or tracks, under a grant of authority from the municipality known as the franchise. Examples of public-service corporations are street-railway companies, telephone and telegraph, gas, water, and lighting companies. Steam railroads, interurban electric railroads, and water-power companies are sometimes included in this classification.

The securities of public-service corporations present desirable opportunities to the investor. Public-service corporations operate in industries which are very profitable, and whose profits are rapidly increasing. Furthermore, owing to the long-standing prejudice of the largest investors against these securities, a prejudice only recently overcome, they can still be purchased at prices which yield between five and six per cent.

It is important to understand why the public-service industries are so exceptionally prosperous. The fact must be admitted. In Philadelphia, for example, the underlying companies of the street-railway system pay extraordinary dividends. The Union Passenger Railway, for example, pays 19 per cent. on its stock, the Thirteenth and Fifteenth Passenger Railway 24 per cent., and the Frankford and Southwark 34 per cent. These are the original underlying companies. While an enormous investment has been made in their property by each of the three companies which have succeeded them in the development of the street-railway system of Philadelphia, yet the large dividends earned by the underlying companies give a good idea of the profits of street-railway operation in a large city. The same may be said of gas, water, telephone, and electric light and power companies. In all large cities, these enterprises are exceedingly profitable.

This statement is made to refer to large cities because it is only in the large city that the operation of the law of increasing returns in public-service industry has reached its full development.

In small cities and towns, public-service industries are no more prosperous than any other.

The operation of the law of increasing returns may be illustrated from the street-railway industry. Street-railway operation involves the maintenance of regular and frequent schedules for the service of the public. It costs but little more to operate a full car than a car half full or empty. Up to the capacity of the tracks in the congested districts, and up to the generating capacity in the power-houses, additional cars may be added to accommodate the increase of traffic with a comparatively small increase in the expense.

The operating expenses of every business include certain items which are comparatively fixed, and certain other items which increase and diminish with the volume of business. A street-railway corporation, for example, makes a certain investment in tracks, overhead work, power houses, car-barns, equipment, and cars. Out of the revenues from the operation of this property, it must earn enough to pay interest on its plant, to keep it in repair, and to provide for its replacement when it is worn out. It must also buy fuel and other supplies, and employ a large number of men in operating its power-house and in keeping its plant in repair. It has an expensive executive and legal staff. It employs, if located in a large city, several thousand motormen and conductors. Out of every five cents which the passenger pays, provision must be made for all of these charges—so much for interest, for depreciation, for maintenance, and for operation of the cars.

The larger the number of people transported by this plant within a given time, the smaller will be the share of these total expenses which must be borne by each passenger, and the larger will be the fraction of the five-cent fare which will remain to the company as its profit. Up to the capacity of its plant, in other words, each additional thousand passengers transported by the street-railway company means a division of the total operating expenses among a larger number of riders, and an increase in the profit which the company takes out of each nickel which the passengers pay.

When the capacity of the plant has been reached, and it becomes necessary to supplement surface street-railway lines costing $60,000 per mile, with elevated lines costing $500,000 per mile, or subway tunnels costing $2,000,000 per mile, then the profits are by no means so great, because the fixed charges have been enormously increased. As soon as this replacement has been made, however, and the traffic, in response to the improved facilities, begins again to increase, the law of increasing returns again comes into operation, and up to the capacity of the new and enlarged plant, each additional thousand passengers means an increase in the margin of profit in each passenger's fare.

The same law controls the expenses and profits of gas, water, and lighting companies. As the population which they serve increases, and the volume of their business grows, it has been found that they can supply this increased demand for long periods without materially increasing their plant, and with comparatively slight increases in operating expenses.

Another feature of the demand for the commodities or service furnished by public-service corporations is that not only does it increase with the growth of population, but that it increases faster than the population grows. The reason for this can be readily understood in the case of the street railway. As the population of a city grows, land values and rentals in the downtown sections rapidly increase. Population, both because of the lower rents in the suburbs, and also because of the cheapness and convenience of transportation which the street railway furnishes, moves from the central sections to the outlying sections. This means that a great number of people live several miles from their work, to which they must go six mornings a week, and from which, six evenings a week, they must return. The larger the population grows, the larger becomes this movement to the outlying sections and the stronger the demand for transportation. The central portion of the city is the natural location for the large department stores, hotels, theatres, and street-railway terminals. These draw in multitudes of people over the street-railway lines.

The same proportionately greater increase in demand, as compared with the growth in population, is seen in the gas industry. From 1890 to 1910, for example, the population of the four boroughs of New York city increased 90.6 per cent. but the consumption of gas increased 164.6 per cent., nearly double the increase in population. In this field, the increase in demand is due not only to the growth of population, but to the growing usefulness of gas in industrial work, as well as for cooking, heating, and other domestic purposes. The business of furnishing light and power and heat shows the same tendency. The investor in the securities of well managed public-service corporations that may be located in a city of at least 100,000 population can be reasonably certain that the city will grow, and that as it grows the profits of his company will increase at a more rapid rate.

Public-service corporations do not, as a rule, divide their earnings with competitors. Even when the city does not give them the exclusive right to supply transportation—and the policy of our law is opposed to exclusive grants of this character—the favorable conditions under which their business is carried on give them a practical monopoly. The nature of this monopoly, as well as the advantages of an investment in a public-service corporation in a large city, was clearly expressed by Mr. Justice Peckham of the United States Supreme Court in delivering the opinion of the court in the case of Wilcox vs. Consolidated Gas Company of New York as follows:

In an investment in a gas company, such as complainants', the risk is reduced almost to a minimum. It is a corporation, which in fact, as the court below remarks, monopolizes the gas service of the largest city in America, and is secure against competition under the circumstances in which it is placed, because it is a proposition *almost unthinkable that the city of New York would, for purposes of making competition, permit the streets of the city to be again torn up in order to allow the mains of another company to be laid all through them to supply gas which the present company can adequately supply.* And, so far as it is given us to look into the future, it seems as certain as anything of such a nature can be, that the demand for gas will increase,—and, at the reduced price, increase to a considerable extent. An interest in such a business is as near a safe and secure investment as can be imagined with regard to any private manufacturing business. . .

In the absence of legal restrictions, a company possessing a monopoly of a necessity of life is limited in its charges only by what the traffic will bear. If the price of gas is too high, the consumption will fall off, and the expense of operation, reversing the process which was explained illustrating the law of diminishing returns, will be increased. Interest, taxes, maintenance, depreciation, executive expenses, advertising, etc., will be spread over a smaller amount of production, and the cost of each thousand feet produced will be correspondingly increased.

It is to the interest of a monopoly to lower the price of its product so far as this lowering of the price will increase consumption and increase profits. Below this point it is not to the interest of the monopoly to go. If, for example, a price of $1.00 per thousand feet will yield $6,000,000 of revenue, while a price of eighty cents will yield a profit of only $5,500,000, because the consumption will not increase to correspond with the reduction in the price, the monopoly, unless constrained by law, will not make the reduction. On the other hand, if a reduction to eighty cents will so much increase the consumption as to raise the profits from $6,000,000 to $7,000,000, it is to the interest of the monopoly to reduce the price. Below the price at which the largest profit will be realized, a corporation having a monopoly of any commodity or service, will not willingly go.

At this point, in the case of the public-service corporation, the State steps in and applies a principle of profit regulation which is as follows: A corporation operating in a public service industry supplying a necessity of life to the community, is entitled to profits equal to a reasonable return on a fair value of its property which is employed in the public service. The fair value of property has been determined, as a result of a long series of judicial decisions, to be a combination of the cost of reproducing and the fair market value of the property at the time the valuation is made. The "reasonable return" depends on circumstances. Again to quote from the Consolidated Gas case:

PUBLIC-SERVICE CORPORATIONS

There is no particular rate of compensation which must in all cases and in all parts of the country be regarded as sufficient for capital invested in business enterprises. Such compensation must depend greatly upon circumstances and locality; among other things, the amount of risk in the business is a most important factor, as well as the locality where the business is conducted and the rate expected and usually realized there upon investments of a somewhat similar nature with regard to the risk attending them. There may be other matters which in some cases might also be properly taken into account in determining the rate which an investor might properly expect or hope to receive, and which he would be entitled to without legislative interference. The less risk, the less right to any unusual returns upon the investments. One who invests his money in a business of a somewhat hazardous character is very properly held to have the right to a larger return without legislative interference, than can be obtained from an investment in Government bonds or other perfectly safe security. The man that invested in gas stock in 1823 had a right to look for and obtain, if possible, a much greater rate upon his investment than he who invested in such property in the city of New York years after the risk and danger involved had been almost entirely eliminated.

In this case, the court found that since the gas business was probably the safest of manufacturing industries, since the Consolidated Gas Company possessed a monopoly, and since its future was reasonably assured, a return of 6 per cent. would be sufficient, and that a price of eighty cents per thousand feet for gas would yield this return.

Starting at 6 per cent. as a "reasonable return" in the safest public-service corporation, we go up in the scale according to circumstances. For ex-

ample, the "reasonable return" for the Great
Northern and Northern Pacific railroads in a
recent court decision was held to be 7 per cent.,
and it is not to be doubted that whenever the
matter comes before the courts for determination
the rate which the public service corporations will
be allowed to earn will be fixed according to the
circumstances of the industry, and of the particular
company in question. A 10 per cent. return
might be reasonable for a street-railway company
in a small city, while it would be exorbitant for a
street railway in a metropolis.

The development of this theory that the public-
service corporation is entitled to no more than a
"reasonable rate of return," while attended with
serious misgiving on the part of bankers and investors when it first came into active application,
is now regarded as one of the greatest safeguards
which the investor in these securities can have.
The public-service corporation is by its nature a
monopoly. If the company is properly capitalized,
if the plant is properly constructed and managed,
and if ordinary business judgment has been used
in fitting the capacity of the plant to the demand
for its product or service, the returns to the investor are certain, because the law allows the

charging of rates which will yield a "reasonable return" on the capital invested. Of no other department of investment is this true. The investor in mining securities, real-estate securities, industrial securities of all kinds, is not given anything by the law. He must take his chances. He has not the advantage of a monopoly. If, as the trusts attempted to do, these enterprises unite to obtain monopolistic power, the law is invoked against them, and these illegal combinations are broken up. The public-service corporation, however, is a monopoly, and the law protects it in the enlargement of its monopolistic profits up to a point of a "reasonable return" which, as has been explained, is quite sufficient to satisfy the investor.

XIII

THE INVESTMENT-BANKER AND THE PUBLIC-UTILITY COMPANY

BONDS of public-service corporations can frequently be bought to yield 5 to 5½ per cent. to the investor. These high yields inspire caution. They raise a presumption against the issue. Cautious investors discriminate against high-yield bonds. High-interest rates and lower prices—are they not indications of lack of demand for these securities? And is not the explanation of this weaker demand a higher percentage of failures in this field than with the railroads? The investment-banker does not waste time in direct answers to these questions. He backs up his offerings of public-service bonds by detailed evidence of their worth, obtained by investigation of every factor influencing their value.

The first step in offering an issue of public-service company bonds, is to investigate the business basis of the proposition, which is found in the territory served. Only large cities or groups of small cities, united for all business purposes, are considered by the best houses for direct offering. When gas, water, electric light, or transportation securities, issued by companies serving small towns, are offered, the usual method is to combine them under a collateral trust mortgage, so that a large issue of bonds, each with the same security, may be offered. I have before me a description of an issue of this character, $9,000,000 in amount, secured by twelve issues of bonds, sundry notes, and fourteen issues of stocks. These securities have a market value of about $22,000,000, and return more than three times the interest on the $9,000,000 bonds. Great difficulty would, however, be met in selling them separately, because of the limited market which would be open to each. The holding company, of which this is an illustration, is useful in making a market for securities of small companies, which would otherwise be unsalable at reasonable prices.

The banker prefers, however, direct offerings of bonds secured not by the pledge of these pieces of paper issued by smaller companies, but by the pledge of property. So far as he is governed by this preference, he must confine his operations to the larger cities, for nowhere else can he find the conditions of perfect security and reasonable certainty of appreciation in value which he desires. His offering is made stronger if the security includes a large amount of surrounding territory, but the foundation must be the dense and growing population of the city. Great importance is placed by the banker upon the growth of the city under examination, not only its past growth in population, but its future as a manufacturing, railroad, and commercial centre. For example, note the following vital facts concerning Seattle, furnished in connection with a recent bond-offering.

In 1880 the population of Seattle was 3,535; in 1890, 42,837; in 1900, 80,671. At present the estimated population is 265,000. From 1903 to 1907 the taxable valuation of the city rose from $56,674,000 to $156,531,724, and bank clearings from $206,913,-000 to $488,591,000. During the past six years, the building permits have increased 300 per cent., and the value of real-estate transfers over 600 per cent. The Great Northern and the Northern Pacific Railway systems have terminals in Seattle, and the Canadian Pacific enters the city. The Chicago, Milwaukee and St. Paul is building to Seattle, and the Union Pacific is planning an entrance from the south. The harbor is excellent. The aggregate commerce of the port in 1907 was $140,472,821. The trade with the Orient and with Alaska, already large, is rapidly increasing. Seattle is 600 miles nearer Yokohama than San Francisco, and the natural gateway for Alaskan trade. Numerous industries are established in the city, which has become undoubtedly the most important business and distributing centre on the North Pacific Coast, and, in fact, one of the great cities of the country.

When such statements can be made concerning a city, and if other conditions affecting security can be satisfactorily met, bonds secured by a lien on its public-service corporation property are as safe as the best railroad bonds.

THE PUBLIC-UTILITY COMPANY

Assuming that the business basis of the company is sound, the next step in the investigation is the engineer's examination. Every banking house of standing has engineering connections, and large sums are often paid for exhaustive reports. The engineer's examination covers the condition of the plant in reference to maintenance and operating efficiency; the quality of the management, especially as to its demonstrated ability to cultivate amicable relations with the public; and the rates charged. If these rates are higher than those generally prevailing in the State, or higher than sufficient to yield a reasonable return upon the investment, they are likely to be reduced; and the bond-issue must be limited accordingly. The engineer also makes a careful appraisal of the cost of replacing the physical property of the company, since this sum represents the figure on which the courts will always allow a reasonable return. The engineer often goes so far as to criticise the policy of the management, to suggest plans for improvement in service, and to point out ways in which the company's business can be expanded. His report is a document often hundreds of pages in length, which gives the banker a complete picture of the property and business which he is asked to finance.

THE CAREFUL INVESTOR

Often, engineering firms, in order to secure constant employment for their organizations, bring propositions to the bankers as promoters, and go so far as to offer their cooperation in financing the undertaking. The tendency is now toward such coöperation between bankers and engineers. A proposition submitted by an engineering concern of standing in its field is sure of respectful and attentive consideration from the banker, who knows that the engineer's primary interest is not to take part in the financing, but to make his regular percentage of engineering profit. The engineer's interest may extend beyond the initial stages of a proposition. He may take charge, for a period, of operating a new concern, breaking in a permanent organization, and insuring economical and efficient management during the trying first years.

Supplementing the engineer's investigation is the audit of the company's books. Banking houses usually employ their own auditors, although they often utilize the services of public accountants. The chief importance of the audit is to make sure that the company's accounts have been properly kept. Many items can be charged to cost of construction which belong in cost of operation. A surplus may be created by placing upon such intangible items as "franchises" a high value which has no substantive basis.

The accountant looks closely to the depreciation charge. As a recent writer on accountancy has well said, "All machinery is on an irresistible march to the junk-heap." Provision must be made out of current income, not only for necessary current replacements, but to provide against the day when a large part of the plant will have to be renewed. All this information is of the greatest interest and value to the banker. He wishes to present to his clients such a statement as the following, and to know that it is accurate.

EARNINGS

(Certified by Messrs. Price, Waterhouse & Company, Chartered Accountants; and Allen Knight, Esq., C. P. A.)

Year ended December 31:	1909.	1910.	1911.
Gross Earnings	$13,491,288	$14,044,596	$14,682,669
Operating expenses, maintenance and taxes	7,531,576	7,921,341	8,151,364
NET EARNINGS	$ 5,959,712	$6,123,255	$ 6,531,305
Bond interest paid			3,278,177
Balance			$ 3,253,128

Gross earnings during the past five years have shown a steady increase, as follows:

1907.	1908.	1909.	1910.	1911.
$11,342,140	$12,657,305	$13,491,288	$14,044,596	$14,682,669

When the banker can submit information of this character, his argument is convincing.

The banker insists upon a large residual value in the property over the amount of the bond-issue. He does not propose to furnish the money to construct his security. The larger this margin of value is, the safer are the bonds. One measure of equity is the market value of stocks, based on dividends paid. The banker is careful, however, to determine whether these dividends have been fully earned; whether the market value upon which he, as the investor's representative, is asked to rely, represents the judgment of the investor or the hopes of the speculator.

A far better guide to the value of the property is the cost of reproduction. That a public-service property has cost $5,000,000 is not conclusive evidence that it can earn interest on this sum. A large part of the money may have been wasted by careless, incompetent engineers, or the plant may be too large for the business to be obtained. As a rule, however, the standard of original cost, or cost of replacement, whichever is the lower, furnishes a safe guide to the "equity" or margin in the property, for the protection of the bonds. With this margin as a starting point, and with the assurance of good management, efficient operation, and the opportunity for the development of a large business, the banker has only one remaining consideration to examine—the franchise.

In a preceding chapter I have shown that public-service companies operating in large cities were so-called natural monopolies, supplying necessities of life to increasing populations at diminishing costs of production and distribution, at prices restricted only by considerations of its own interest. These opportunities for large profit must, however, be enjoyed under the supervision of the State. Unreasonable rates will not be permitted. The evidence of unreasonable rates is found in an unusually high percentage of earnings. If the corporation has an express franchise contract with the city, permitting it to charge a certain price or fare, it cannot be disturbed, no matter how great may be its profits. In the absence of such a stipulation, the company's earnings may at any time be reduced to what the courts consider a reasonable return, by a change in rates, fares, or prices.

The banker must look closely into the franchise question. He must consider first the term. If the franchise is for 25 years, then the bonds which he buys should mature within 25 years. The banker next considers the burdens imposed by the franchise upon the company, what payments— car licenses, street repairs, lighting, direct contribution to the public treasury—does it impose, and finally, what are the provisions for extension at the expiration of the franchise? These questions are the most important asked by the banker concerning the terms on which the company, the purchase of whose bonds he is considering, will be allowed to do business during the life of the bonds.

In recent years a solution of the franchise question has been attempted by the development of various plans of city partnership in public-service undertakings. The experiments of Chicago, Philadelphia and New York in this direction we have now to consider.

XIV

THE PUBLIC-SERVICE CORPORATION AND THE CITY

THE last chapter outlined the examination which is made by the investment-banker when he is asked to purchase the securities of a public-service corporation. The conclusion was reached that the most important part of this examination concerns the franchise, the right of the company to do business.

The foundation of investment is legal security. A corporation is created by the State, and is protected by the power which creates it. It is given great privileges: the right to do business as a private individual or a partnership; the right to take private property at a fair valuation even against the will of its owners; the right to occupy the public streets with tracks, pipes, and wires; and the right to a fair return on the money which its owners have contributed, or which it may have borrowed from creditors.

Along with these rights, however, go certain obligations, often not clearly defined in charters and franchise contracts, but more or less clearly understood by all parties. These obligations are to give good service, to charge reasonable rates, to seek additional privileges only through legitimate channels, to recognize that a public corporation has a public duty to perform, and that the interests of the people are, in a sense, placed in its keeping.

The case is perfectly plain. Here is an agreement to which the public and the public-service corporations are parties. The party of the first part gives certain privileges, special opportunities for making money. The party of the second part, perhaps not expressly, but by plain implication, agrees to develop these privileges and opportunities in such a way as to benefit not merely themselves but the people from whom these advantages are derived.

There is a widespread sentiment, only recently beginning to subside, that the public-service corporations have not lived up to their part of the agreement. It is claimed, and generally believed, that these valuable franchise privileges have been capitalized at excessive figures, and that unreasonable rates and prices have been charged to pay interest and dividends on this inflated capitalization. As a result of this heavy capitalization, which often takes the form of bonds or is represented by leases at very high figures, it is claimed that the good service which should be rendered by the public-service corporation is frequently allowed to deteriorate. In other words, in order to pay interest, dividends, and rentals, the public is forced to stand in the street-cars, when a more moderate capitalization would allow a sufficient equipment to give each rider a seat.

There was, no doubt, some ground for these criticisms, even though the statements on which they were based were in many cases greatly exaggerated and distorted.

Within the last ten years the public came to believe that they were absolved from their implied promise to allow the public-service corporations a free hand in their business, since the public-service corporations had not kept their part of the agreement. The aid of the government was thereupon invoked to force what the people considered restitution. Taxes were laid upon franchises. The price of gas and telephone service was subjected to sudden and drastic reduction. Public sentiment was invoked to refuse to extend franchise grants, and taxes on property were largely in-

creased. Restrictions, as, for example, in reference to street cleaning and repair, or the placing
of wires underground, were imposed. In many
parts of the country—Chicago, Cleveland, St.
Louis, Detroit, Pittsburg, Philadelphia, and New
York—this agitation against the public-service
corporations broke out with great violence. The
agitation resulted, for a time, in discrediting the
securities of these companies. As a result several
of these corporations were forced into bankruptcy.
Others staggered along on the brink of insolvency.
It was impossible to obtain the capital for necessary improvements and extensions in the face of
hostile public opinion. The investor would have
nothing to do with securities which were so badly
tainted with unpopularity.

The situation became intolerable. On the one
hand, the public was suffering from the lack of the
facilities, particularly in the field of transportation; on the other hand, companies could not raise
the money to provide these facilities. The people
attacked the corporations for their bad service, and
the corporations responded, with truth, that until
the attitude of the public changed and these attacks
ceased, bad service was all that could be furnished.
A compromise was demanded in every interest.

THE CITY

One of the best evidences of the essential sanity of the American people in their dealings with the problems of public business is the manner in which they have worked out, to a satisfactory solution, the problems of the relations between the city and the public-service corporation. How this has been done can best be told by a series of illustrations.

The Chicago Railways Company owns and operates about 450 miles of electric railway, serving the downtown sections as well as the entire north and west sides of the city of Chicago. This company is the successor of two corporations which formerly operated these properties, and which, in their turn, represented consolidations of smaller companies. All these companies were greatly overcapitalized, and the service which they furnished was perhaps the worst in the United States.

As a result of negotiations with the city of Chicago, which followed the refusal of the city to extend the franchises of the companies, an ordinance was passed dated February 11, 1907, and approved by the voters, which granted the Chicago Railways Company a twenty-year franchise. Under this franchise ordinance, the company was required to carry out a comprehensive plan of rebuilding the property. During the next two years, the company spent about $29,000,000 on these improvements, and the property, on February 1, 1911, was appraised at $68,226,612. The city retains an option to purchase all of the properties of the company for municipal ownership and operation at any time during the life of the franchise at a price equal to the valuation on February 1, 1907, $30,779,875, plus all expenditures since February 1, 1907, for reconstruction and extensions.

In case the property shall not be purchased before the expiration of the twenty years named in the franchise, the city agrees that it will not then grant a franchise to any other corporation for a competing system of street railways in this company's territory, unless this corporation shall purchase the property of the company at the price specified. The city may require the company to sell this property to some other corporation or may purchase it itself prior to 1927, but in either case the price paid shall be 20 per cent. above the $30,779,875, the original appraised value, plus the cost of the cost of all additions. The franchise further provides for a straight five-cent fare, with universal transfer.

An important feature of the agreement is the

division of the earnings. For the first time, a large American municipality asserted its right to participate in the profits of companies owning and occupying its streets for the purpose of profit. The agreement provides that out of the gross earnings of the company there shall first be paid all taxes and fixed charges for maintaining the property and replacing it, and 5 per cent. upon the value of the properties as increased from time to time. What remains is called surplus earnings. Of these earnings, the city is entitled to 55 per cent. and the company to 45 per cent.

This contract has proven to be profitable for the city, and it is expected that in time it will be profitable for the company. For the year 1911–12, the net income from the operation of these lines was $1,494,375. Of this amount the city of Chicago received, as its share in the municipal enterprise, $821,906, and the company received $672,469. The company has excellent credit, and its property has been completely reconstructed, all this work being done under the supervision of a Board of Supervising Engineers responsible to the city. The service is now excellent.

In spite of the fact that the bonds of this company are issued under what is known as an open-end mortgage—that is, a mortgage which places no limit upon the amount of bonds to be issued—the careful supervision of the expenditure of the proceeds of the bonds, and the great security which the investor feels in the contract with the city of Chicago, has maintained prices for these bonds, which, when one considers the large amount issued, and the unsavory reputation of Chicago traction securities before the passage of this ordinance, must be regarded as remarkably high.

The settlement of the transit problem in Philadelphia proceeded along different lines, although the same underlying principle of partnership between the city and the company was followed. The street-railway system of Philadelphia had been controlled since July 1, 1902, by the Philadelphia Rapid Transit Company. This company succeeded in operation and control to the Union Traction Company, which was the successor of three former consolidations. The method of consolidation in each case was a lease of the underlying companies to a controlling company at a high rate.

These successive increases in rentals from one consolidation to another were paid without difficulty so long as the street-railway system was operated by surface lines. The population grew

steadily, and the earnings rapidly increased.
When the Rapid Transit Company entered the
field, however, it became necessary to invest a
great sum in an elevated and subway property,
to build additional power plants, and to replace
a large amount of track and equipment. The
Rapid Transit Company spent, approximately,
$50,000,000 on the system. In spite of this enor-
mous outlay, however, the profits did not increase.
Many complaints were also made of the inadequacy of the service furnished by the company.
It was proposed that the city should exercise the
reserved right of purchasing the company's property, that franchises should be granted to competing companies if they would agree to good service,
and that the company should be forced to place
its overhead wires in underground conduits. These
persistent attacks upon the company seriously
injured its credit, and transportation development was at a standstill.

Under the inspiration of an association of retail
merchants, in 1907, the year that marked the conclusion of the Chicago agreement, the relations
between the Rapid Transit Company and the
city of Philadelphia were adjusted by an agreement. This agreement provided for a community

of interest between the city and the company. The company agrees that it will not make any issues of stocks or bonds without first obtaining the approval of the city; that if the city shall at any time decide that new lines should be built, it shall notify the company to build such new lines, and if the company does not accept the plans of the city in this respect, the city may offer the right to construct such roads to any other corporation; that the mayor and two citizens shall represent the city on the board; and that the city is to share equally with the company in all dividends above the return of 6 per cent. to the share-holders, which, however, since no dividends have been paid, stands as an accumulated charge in favor of the stock-holders and against the city; that the company relinquishes its right to build a subway bisecting the city from north to south, allowing the city to make any other arrangement which may seem desirable for its construction; and that the company shall maintain a sinking fund which, beginning July 1, 1912, shall amount to $120,000 a year for ten years, and shall thereafter increase until $5,000,000 has been accumulated, which shall then be paid into the city treasury, and all future sinking fund payments made to the city treasurer.

In addition to the sinking-fund payments, the company, during the first ten years, in lieu of all obligations for paving, removal of snow, license fees, etc., shall pay into the city treasury the sum of $500,000, this increasing until, during the last ten years of the agreement, it shall reach $700,000. On July 1, 1957, or on any July 1 thereafter, the city reserves the right to purchase all the property, leaseholds, and franchises of the company for an amount equal to the par value of its capital stock outstanding, at the date of agreement $30,000,000, plus any additional stock issued with the consent of the city. The money paid into the sinking fund is to be available to the city in part purchase of the property of the company, should the city elect to exercise its option.

Upon the acceptance by the company of this agreement, the city confirmed all of the franchises and rights of the company and its subsidiaries, many of which had been called into serious question, and provided that the rates of fare then obtaining could be changed only with the consent of both parties.

This agreement finally laid to rest all the apprehensions of investors in Philadelphia street-railway stocks and bonds as to the legal security of their investment. It made the city and the company partners in their transportation system. It gave the city what will eventually be a substantial interest in the properties of the company. It insured a large measure of control by the city officials over certain features of the management of the company. It made provision for the future growth of the system by the construction of additional lines. It also reserved to the city the right to acquire a property which in 1957 will be enormously valuable, at a price which is reasonably certain to represent but a portion of its value.

New York City has gone still further in the harmonizing of the relations between the city and the public-service corporation. New York has worked out a plan for utilizing the credit of the city in the construction of subway lines for which private capital could not be secured on advantageous terms. In the case of the original subway, the city furnished all the money for construction. Large extensions of this system are now in progress, which will be paid for in part by the companies and in part with public money. The leases and contracts under which the city furnishes this money are made on terms which provide for the payment of interest on the city bonds issued to provide these funds, plus a sinking fund. The right of purchase at the end of a term of years is reserved. They represent the furthest development in the coöperation between the city and the municipality.

The rights of the public either to own their transportation system or to retain the reserved interest, and, in the meantime, to share in the profits; to supervise, in so far as is necessary to secure good service, construction and operation; and to regulate the capitalization to prevent inflation, are now established. In return, the public has come to recognize its obligation to protect the companies in the enjoyment of liberal franchise privileges for a fixed term of years, to secure adequate compensation for all their outlay of capital; and, at the end of the franchise period, in case it is not deemed wise to extend these privileges, to pay to the company a fair compensation for the property. Finally, if New York is to be taken as the most advanced type of municipal coöperation with public-service corporations it is now recognized as a proper function of municipal government, to provide, by the use of the public credit, for the construction of subway lines, which are then to be turned over for operation to private

175

corporations. The public-service corporations, in their turn, have not only recognized the right of the people to ownership and control, but also to share in the profits of operation.

Ten years ago there was much talk of municipal ownership and operation of public utilities as the only escape from a situation which, all agreed, was fast becoming intolerable. To-day, while municipal ownership, actual or reserved, is now accepted without question, the talk of municipal operation has entirely disappeared. The American city and the public-service corporation have entered into a partnership for mutual advantage. As a result of this partnership, the position of public-service corporations before the public and with the investor has been much improved.

XV

THE PUBLIC-SERVICE COMMISSION AND THE INVESTOR [1]

WE have examined the methods employed by the investment-banker in investigating the securities of public-service corporations. We saw with what great care these investigations are made, and with what searching scrutiny every factor bearing upon the merits of the enterprise is considered. As a result of these careful examinations, the number of failures among public-utility corporations is each year diminishing, and the investor can buy these securities with confidence.

Supplementing the work of the investment-banker, although undertaken with a different motive, many States have established administrative bodies known as Public-Service Commissions, who are charged with the duty of supervising the rates and prices, the service, and, incidentally, the capitalization, accounting methods, and financial policy of public-service corporations. The primary

---

[1] NOTE.—This chapter is substantially identical with Chapter VI in the author's Corporation Finance.

object in the establishment of these commissions has been to protect the public against bad service and excessive rates and prices.

In order to make sure that corporations subject to their jurisdiction are honestly capitalized, so that they may not have any inducement unduly to advance rates in order to pay interest and dividends on capitalization representing no actual value, and in order that the proceeds of their sales of stock and bonds should be applied to the improvement of their plant and to the consequent betterment of their service, some of the Public-service Commission laws clothe the commissions with authority over the issue of securities.

The nature of this power over security issues is indicated by the following extract from the Act Creating the Public-Service Commissions of New York:

Any common carrier, railroad corporation or street railroad corporation organized under the laws of the State of New York, may issue bonds, stocks, notes or other evidences of indebtedness payable at periods of more than twelve months after the date thereof, when necessary for the acquisition of property, the construction, completion, extension or improvement of its facilities, or for the improvement or maintenance of its service or for the discharge or lawful refunding of its obligations, provided and not otherwise that there shall have been secured from the proper commission an order authorizing such issue, and the amount thereof and stating that, in the opinion of the commission, the use of the capital to be secured by the issue of such stock, bonds, notes, or other evidences of indebtedness is reasonably required for the said purpose of the corporation. For the purpose of enabling it to determine whether it should issue such an order, the commission shall make such inquiry or investigation, hold such hearings and examine such witnesses, books, papers, documents or contracts as it may deem of importance in enabling it to reach a determination.

Under this power, every corporation proposing to issue or authorize any securities must apply to the Public-Service Commission for authorization, and the new securities will not be sanctioned unless the Commission is first satisfied that the issue is for the best interests of the company. The method of procedure in cases involving the authorization of bond-issues is outlined by the Commission of the Second District of New York in its second annual report, as follows:

In passing upon the application for leave to issue additional capital stock, the Commission will consider:

Whether there is reasonable prospect of fair return upon the investment proposed, to the end that securities having apparent worth but actually little or no value may not be issued with our sanction.

We think that to a reasonable extent the interests of the investing public should be considered by us in passing upon these applications.

The Commission should satisfy itself that, in a general way, the venture will be likely to prove commercially feasible, but it should not undertake to reach and announce a definite conclusion that the new construction or improvement actually constituted a safe or attractive basis for investment. Commercial enterprises depend for their success upon so many conditions which cannot be foreseen or reckoned with in advance, that the duty of the Commission is discharged as to applications of this character when it has satisfied itself that the contemplated purpose is a fair business proposition.

Although the Commission here expressly disaffirms its intention to guarantee the securities whose issues it sanctions, yet its method of procedure is so careful as actually to reach this result. This method is as follows:

An estimate will be made from a consideration of the results of operation of existing roads of the probable gross earnings.

An estimate will be made in like manner of the probable operating expenses, taxes, and depreciation charges.

The excess of earnings over the disbursements which must be made before fixed charges can be met represents the sum which is applicable to fixed charges.

The maximum bond issue which will be allowed must be determined by the sum thus ascertained to be applicable to the payment of the interest charge.

No bond issue should be permitted creating an interest charge beyond an amount which it is reasonably certain can be met from the net earnings.

Stock representing a cash investment should be required to an amount sufficient to afford a moral guarantee that, in the judgment of those investing, the enterprise is likely to prove commercially successful.

The order authorizing such stock and bond issues will contain approximate provisions designed to secure the construction of the road in accordance with the plans and specifications upon which the authorization was made and not in excess of the actual requirements.

THE INVESTOR

If the allowance proves inadequate for the required purposes, an application for further capitalization may be made, upon which application the expenditure of the proceeds of stock and bonds already authorized must be shown in detail.

After an issue of bonds has passed successfully through the ordeal of this investigation, the investor need have little fear concerning their safety.

There is another aspect of the Public-Service Commission matter which is even more reassuring to the investor. When a Public-Service Commission has authorized the issue of securities, it is, by implication, bound to protect the company whose application it has authorized, not merely against the action of their directors in borrowing money or issuing stock against the best interests of the corporation, but also to protect them against competing enterprises for which there is no public necessity, and which would not, therefore, prove profitable. The best recent example of the protection which the Public-Service Commission gives a company whose capitalization and rates are subject to its jurisdiction, is in the refusal of the application of the Buffalo, Rochester and Eastern Railroad for authority to issue securities for the construction of a line of railroad from Buffalo to Albany which was to parallel the line of the New

York Central. The ground of the refusal was that there was no necessity for the new line, that it would not prove profitable, that it would injure the New York Central, and that no public benefit would result. A summary of the conclusions of the Commission upon these various matters is as follows:

First, that the cost of the proposed road would be about $100,000,000.

Second, that existing railroad facilities between Buffalo and the Hudson River were adequate to take care of existing business and for a very large increase in future traffic.

Third, that the cost of the proposed road would require a capitalization of $336,700 per mile, much larger than the capitalization of any railroad system in the country.

Fourth, that this capitalization would require earnings per mile of at least $48,100, if 5 per cent. was to be earned on the amount invested.

Fifth, that to earn this sum would involve a traffic greatly in excess of the traffic of any railroad in the country.

Sixth, that the proposed road would not be able to forward its freight over its eastern connections at the Hudson River, since these were already over-taxed.

THE INVESTOR

Seventh, that the proposed road did not contemplate any benefit to the public in the reduction of rates, and, finally, that the applicant had not shown sufficient financial ability to justify issuing to it a certificate of public convenience and necessity to construct a road costing $100,000,000.

If the Public Service Commission of New York had been in existence thirty years ago, the unnecessary, costly, and wasteful West Shore and Nickel Plate Railroads, which were constructed for no other purpose than to divide traffic which the New York Central and the Lake Shore and Michigan Southern were handling with economy and despatch, would not have been authorized, and a large amount of the reckless railroad construction west of the Mississippi, which bankrupted the Atchison, Topeka and Santa Fe, the St. Louis and San Francisco, and assisted in breaking down the Northern Pacific, would not have been sanctioned.

The Public-Service Commission not only protects the investor against the inevitable consequences of competition where no necessity for the competing property exists, but it also secures his company in the right to charge such rates and fares as will yield a reasonable return on securities.

THE CAREFUL INVESTOR

At the time the New York Public-Service Commissions were instituted, the most serious apprehensions were expressed by financial interests that the new laws which took from directors and stockholders most of the control which they had previously exercised over the issues of new securities would seriously interfere with the efforts of companies to provide new capital. As the Commissions have progressed, however, since they have been forced into the position of virtually guaranteeing every issue which they approve on the basis of a careful investigation of the prospects of the enterprise, a critical examination of its engineering features, the rock on which so many new schemes are wrecked, and an assurance to the investor that reasonable rates will be allowed and that cut-throat competition will be prevented, they have come to be very favorably regarded by investment bankers.

The bond-salesman who can offer a security whose issue has been approved by some public-service commission has his work of persuasion largely accomplished. Indeed, the sentiment among investment-bankers is nearly unanimous as to the benefits which have come to their business from the work of these regulative bodies.

XVI

FARM MORTGAGES

A FARM mortgage does not differ from any other mortgage. It is a promise to pay one, two, five, or ten thousand dollars in three or five years from date, and it is secured by the mortgage which conveys, in trust, to the lender the title to the mortgaged property. This conveyance is recorded in the county in which the property is located, thus establishing the claim of the lender as a first lien upon the mortgaged premises. The advantages and disadvantages of this form of mortgage, as compared with an investment in the bonds of a large corporation, may be summarized as follows:

The first advantage of the farm mortgage is its high yield. The Central West, the part of the country in which mortgage loans are preferably made by conservative investors, is now making loans on a 6 per cent. basis to the investor. The Western States, as a rule, do not tax at home investments in foreign loans, and this gives the investor the opportunity to realize the full interest return.

The second advantage of the farm loan is its early maturity. The purchaser of a bond of a railway company cannot get his money back from the company for, perhaps, thirty or even fifty years. His only way of recovering his principal is to sell his bond to some other investor. This involves the risk of depreciation in the principal. The investor may have purchased his bond for 105, and when he comes to sell, it may have declined to 99½, owing to a falling-off in the demand for securities of that character. The bond is still perfectly good, his interest will be paid regularly, but he has sustained a loss on the capital value of his investment. The investor in a farm mortgage, however, can get his money back from the borrower at the end of three or five years.

The third point in favor of the farm mortgage is closely connected with that just mentioned, namely, the greater control which the investor has over his investment. Provision is usually made in the mortgage for an indefinite extension from year to year at the expiration of the term named in the instrument. When this provision is included, if the investor wishes the return of his principal at the end of the term, he can have it. If he wishes a longer-term investment, he can allow the mortgage to run from year to year. A good farmer can make more than 6 per cent. by investing money in buildings and improvements and in land, and often is not anxious to pay off his mortgage. At the end of any year, however, the mortgage can be called up and the investor can get his money.

All mortgages, moreover, whether issued by a great railway company or by a small farmer in North Dakota, provide that the borrower should keep his farm, which is the lender's security, in good condition and the buildings in good repair. It is almost impossible for the investor in a corporation bond to enforce these provisions. He is only one of perhaps 2,000 bond-holders; he is represented by a trustee, and he must rely upon the trustee to enforce the terms of the mortgage. It is not the custom for the trustee, whatever powers may be given him by the mortgage instrument, to interfere with the management of the company. Instances have occurred where the security of mortgage bonds has been seriously impaired because of long-continued neglect of the property. This is not possible with the farm mortgage, or with any other form of real-estate obligation, where the security of each loan is a single piece of property, and where the investor has the opportunity of inspection.

Against these advantages of farm-mortgage loans, certain disadvantages are urged. Some of these disadvantages are inherent in this form of obligation; others can be overcome by employing the services of reputable mortgage-brokers. The first point urged against the farm mortgage is its short duration. At the end of a few years, the lender may have his money handed back to him, and be obliged to look for a new investment. In practice, however, this objection is not serious. Either the mortgage is allowed to run from year to year, or a new investment of equal security can be obtained without difficulty.

Then, too, it is urged against the farm mortgage, that the application of the proceeds of the mortgage to productive purposes is not safeguarded as it is in a bond executed by a corporation. When a railroad company, for example, puts out an issue of bonds whose proceeds are to cover the construction of a branch line, the bonds will not be issued by the trustee to the banking house except upon the certificate of the company's engineer that a certain amount of mileage has been constructed. Not until the whole improvement has been completed, will the entire number of bonds be issued. In corporation mortgages, the attempt is always made to provide for the productive expenditure of the proceeds of the bonds. "Spendthrift borrowing" is not possible.

With farm mortgages this safeguard is not usually provided. The security is stated, but the purposes to which the money is to be applied are not given. In a number of applications for farm loans which I have before me, no questions are asked concerning the use which the borrower will make of these funds, nor is any attempt made to condition the payment of the money upon the certificate of some third party that a certain investment of the money is assured. This information can usually be obtained by the investor, however, either through the broker or, if he lends the money in person, from the borrower. There is no reason why farm-mortgage loans should not be strengthened by providing this very important safeguard.

The objection is often made to farm mortgages that they are not available for either quick sale or as collateral. This objection is, in the main, well founded. Farm mortgages share this defect, however, with many unlisted bonds. Bonds secured by first mortgage on a property of a small gas company, for example, have a very slow and uncertain market, and are only available for collateral at institutions where the property and the borrower are well known. If the investor in Massachusetts buys a farm mortgage secured on lands in North Dakota, his only method of selling the mortgage is to place it through a broker, who will charge him a commission for selling it. He can also use it as collateral about as well as he could use an unlisted bond at a bank or trust company where his character and standing are well known, but whose officers are not familiar with the value of the property securing the bonds.

The availability of farm mortgages as collateral is also restricted by the prohibition in the national banking law against lending on real-estate mortgages. This prohibition does not apply, however, to loans by many other financial institutions.

It must be admitted that the farm mortgage has a slower market than the corporation bond, although it can be sold through the same channels as those through which it was purchased. It is also not easy to borrow upon farm mortgages. These objections, however, apply only to the mortgage as a business man's investment. To the investor who is looking for a safe place for his money, who does not expect to sell, and who does not need to borrow, this argument against the farm mortgage does not apply. There is, finally, the objection to the Western farm mortgage from the standpoint of the Eastern investor, that the lender is sending his money often 2,000 miles away, lending it to a man whom he has never seen, on the security of property which he will never view, and taking a variety of risks and hazards, for example, of drought, sickness, etc., from which an investment in corporation or municipal bonds is entirely free.

It is this situation which calls the mortgage-broker into existence. Without his intervention, it would be impossible for the eastern investor to put his money into Western farm mortgages. The experienced and reliable mortgage-broker, however, who is merely an investment-banker in a specialized field, is able to remove these objections to mortgage loans.

An outline of the service which the broker performs for the investor will show how indispensable this service is. I take this description from a booklet issued by a mortgage company doing business in a Northwestern State, and which has been in business for 34 years, with whose standing I am personally acquainted, and for the accuracy of whose statements I can vouch. The amount of loans offered for investment by this company are usually from 30 to 40 per cent. of the actual market value of the loan. The term of the loan is five years. When desired by the borrower, the privilege is extended of repayment of part of the loan with interest date. Such repayment increases the margin of security in the property, and the money can be reinvested in other mortgages if desired. The average size of the loan is about $2,000. These loans are made by the company with its own money after personal examinations of the property.

The method of making farm loans is as follows: The farmer wishes to borrow money for additional buildings, for the purchase of live stock, or for payment for land. He makes application to the company for a loan secured on his land. His application furnishes complete information about his land, his equipment, buildings, live stock, and machinery, as well as personal information about himself, his farm, his neighbors, and general neighborhood conditions in his locality.

Of special interest in this connection is the detailed information which is obtained concerning the borrower. Some of these questions are extremely personal. The following is a specimen list:

1. Full name and age of borrower.
2. Married or single.
3. Full name and age of wife.
4. If formerly married, state wife's full name and whether divorced or deceased.
5. If deceased, state whether she left a will, and if so when and where the same is probated.
6. If divorced, state where the decree is filed.
7. State name, sex, ages, and residences of children by divorced wife.
8. Have you any who are dependent upon you aside from your own family?
9. What is the general physical condition of your family?
10. Give name, sex, and age of your children.
11. What ones live at home with you?
12. Husband born where?
13. Wife born where?
14. Belong to church?
15. Belong to fraternal societies?
16. Politics?
17. Do you drink, and if so to what extent?

The purpose of obtaining this detailed information is both for the sake of security and that the prospective investor may have an accurate knowledge of the character of the man to whom he is lending his money. It also assists the attorneys for the mortgage company in searching the title.

From this information, the loan committee of the company passes judgment on the loan applied for. If it is approved, the information is, as far as possible, verified on the ground by their own examiner. The title to the property is then examined by their attorneys. If found perfect, papers for signature and amount agreed upon as a safe loan are sent to their agent for the final settlement, and the mortgage is recorded at the county seat. The complete papers are then assembled and, after proper record is made, are given a mortgage number and become a part of the investment. The papers in a mortgage envelope consist of note and mortgage, assignment of mortgage, abstract of title, insurance policy, if any, application and examiner's report. The mortgage company guarantees each title.

The mortgage company not only makes a careful investigation of the quality of the mortgage, but during the period of investigation it assumes the entire management of the loan. A record is kept which enables the company to ascertain whether the farmer's taxes and insurance premiums are promptly paid, and to collect his interest, as well as the principal sum, when due. This provision is made without expense to the owner of the mortgage, and the company's profit, moreover, is paid by the borrower.

FARM MORTGAGES

Two illustrations of the mortgages offered by this concern will show the quality of the security which is furnished. The names are fictitious:

JAMES W. BROWN

$2,000 ———————— County, North Dakota.

This mortgage is dated December 1, 1910, and is due December 1, 1915. The loan is secured upon N. E. ¼ 30–133–62, 140 acres under cultivation and 20 acres fenced to pasture. It is otherwise improved by a set of buildings costing $1,200 or $1,300, carrying insurance for $800. The borrower has stock and machinery sufficient to run his farm, and is worth about $3,000 all clear of encumbrances. The soil is a rich, heavy black loam, with clay sub-soil. This quarter, I think, would readily sell at $45 or $50 an acre. The land is situated about 5½ miles from ————————, and the loan is being made to pay a loan now on the land.

C. F. EVERHARDT

$4,500 ———————— County.

This mortgage is secured upon 280 acres of land about five miles north and west from ————————. The borrower is a German, and has resided here more than twenty years. 160 acres of the land are now under cultivation and the balance fenced to pasture. It is otherwise improved by buildings costing $2,500. I do not believe that the land could be bought for less than $50 an acre. It is a loan that I can recommend in the highest terms.

Loans made on this character of security are not open to question. When the broker is reliable—and the investor can usually ascertain this fact through his local bank—so that his statements can be relied upon, an investment in a farm mortgage is as safe as an investment in any other form of security. The farm-mortgage investor has the advantage of a high-interest rate, and, if this is an object to him, an early maturity of his loan. Against this higher rate must be balanced the slower market and the greater difficulty in borrowing on the mortgage, as compared with a mortgage bond of first quality.

XVII

THE MORTGAGE BANK

PRODUCTIVE land furnishes the ultimate security for the investor. Outside of the mining industry, which contributes but little to the supply of investment securities, all other forms of investment rest directly or indirectly upon the farms. Railway traffic mainly comes from the farms. The farms furnish most of the raw material of manufacture. As yet, however, there has been little realization of the farms themselves as a basis of investment. The railroads of the United States are worth, in round numbers, $20,000,000,000. This entire value is outstanding in the hands of the investors in the form of stocks and bonds. The amount of securities issued by industrial corporations is probably greater than the value of the property which these companies own. Public-service corporations are fully represented by investment securities. It is only in the field of real estate, however, and particularly farm real estate, that investments still lag far behind value.

According to the census, there are in the United

States 6,361,502 farms, containing a total of
878,798,000 acres. The total value of this farm
property is estimated at $40,991,000,000, of which
over two-thirds represents the value of the land,
one-sixth the value of the buildings, and one-sixth
the combined value of the improvements, machinery, and live stock. The total value of this farm
property has more than doubled during the decade
1900 to 1910. The increase in farm land alone has
been 118.1 per cent. The average value per acre of
the American farm increased from $15.57 in 1900,
to $32.40 in 1910. The explanation of this phenom-
enal increase in land values is found in the fact that
while the total population increased 21 per cent.
since 1900, the urban population increased 34.8 per
cent. and the rural population only 11.2 per cent.
The number and acreage of farms increased much
less rapidly than the total population. The value
of farm products, as a consequence of this steadily
growing demand from cities and towns for food
supply, has been rapidly advancing, and has made
agriculture easily a most profitable business.

This great industry, however, is but little known
to the investor. The savings banks and insurance
companies, and, to a less extent, the commercial
banks and trust companies, have realized the

value of the perfect security which the farm mortgage offers, but to the individual investor in the East these advantages are almost unknown.

It is unfortunate for the United States that this is the case. The great problem before the American people to-day is the rising cost of living. However economists may wrangle about the ultimate underlying cause of the advance of the price of bread and meat, the plain explanation of this fact is that there is too little bread and too little meat. The only cure for the high prices of food is to produce more food. The production of food is largely a matter of the investment of capital. The time of free land with soil six feet deep, which would produce 20 crops of grain in succession without fertilizer, is past. An extension of the farms in the United States to-day means costly improvement in drainage and irrigation, large expenditures on improved farm buildings, farm machinery, fertilizer, and improved live stock.

The total area of lands in the United States which are to be reclaimed in whole or in part by drainage is estimated at 225,000,000 acres. Of this amount, 75,000,000 acres are in swamps entirely unproductive, while 150,000,000 acres include land whose productivity could be increased at least 20 per cent. by drainage. This is equal to the combined area of Germany, Great Britain, Belgium, and Holland. It is estimated that this area would sustain a population of 125,000,000, and would add $4,000,000,000 a year to the public wealth of the United States. In Florida alone 18,000,000 acres of land can be reclaimed by drainage.

These impressive figures give some idea of the problem before the American farmer and the American consumer. The farmer must have more capital. Mr. James J. Hill, a few years ago, aroused much discussion by the statement that the railroads of the United States required a capital investment of $1,000,000,000 a year for at least five years in order to fit them to handle economically the traffic which would be offered. The needs of the railroads are insignificant compared with the needs of the farms. The crying need of the United States to-day is for larger investment in agriculture.

The need of a large investment in farm mortgages is great. Without this investment, the problem of the future food supply is certain to grow more and more perplexing. And yet, with the present machinery of farm investment, it is unreasonable to expect any large increase in the movement of money into this field. The method of investment in the farm mortgage has already been explained. The investor in Pennsylvania or in New York must lend $3,000, $5,000, or $10,000 to a man in Oklahoma or Nebraska or North Dakota whom he has never seen, and whom he knows only through the statements made to him by the broker. This loan is for a limited time. At the end of that time, he fears that his money may be handed back to him, and he will have to make a new investment, shifting and changing from one thing to another. If he deals with reliable brokers whose names he can readily obtain through his local bank, he runs, it is true, no risk of loss, but the form of the investment does not commend itself to him.

The Eastern investor is accustomed to purchasing stocks and bonds of the large railroad and industrial and public-service corporations, issued in $50,000,000, $100,000,000, and $200,000,000 lots. He buys standard securities—issued by wealthy corporations with whose operations and history he has long been familiar, and which he regards as permanent institutions. It is natural that he should prefer 4½ and 5 per cent. income from a railway bond or railway stock issued by such companies, to 6 per cent. on a farm mortgage.

This prejudice in favor of standard securities will not soon be overcome. The farm-mortgage business has been vigorously pushed for many years, and yet other fields of investment which have been recently opened, such, for example, as the industrials, have absorbed several billions of dollars which it would have been to the national interest to put into farm mortgages. The farm-mortgage broker, with his present organization, cannot win the favor of the investor. If the farm mortgage is to reach the position which it deserves, the organization of the business must be changed, the institution of the mortgage bank must be established in this country.

The mortgage bank is well known in every country of Western Europe. In Germany, as a recent investigation showed, there were 36 mortgage banks with capital of $170,563,000 and combined reserves of $66,711,400. These banks had $2,618,-000 loaned out on mortgage. Against these mortgages and to obtain the money for this investment, the banks had issued $2,548,000,000 in bonds. Of this amount $1,571,000,000 were 4 per cent. bonds and $977,000,000 were 3½ and

3¼ per cent. The German mortgage banks, by standardizing the farm mortgage, have been able to sell their bonds on better terms than the American railroads can obtain for their first-mortgage securities.

The mortgage bank gathers together thousands of individual loans, consolidates them into one aggregate security, and upon this security issues a standard bond. In addition to the security of the mortgages, there is the capital and accumulated earnings of the banks. The same institution, although less highly developed, is found in France, Russia, Austria, Italy, and, more recently, in Great Britain.

From the standpoint of the borrower, the mortgage bank offers great advantages. The American method of borrowing on farm security is to make a short-term loan from three to five years. At maturity, this loan is often reduced or paid off, and money which should properly go into the development of the farm is used to reduce the loan. If the loan cannot be paid off, a new loan must be placed, and this means a commission and material increase in the expense. A farmer who renews his mortgage from time to time is fortunate to escape with a total cost of 7½ per cent. on the money which he obtains, and, on this account, the farm mortgage is always looked upon as a burden which often becomes a curse.

We find nothing of this kind in the railway field. Railway bonds are never paid off. When they come due, they are refunded into new bonds. The investor does not wish his money back; he merely wishes security for his income. As long as security can be furnished him, he knows that he can obtain the amount of his principal from some other investor to whom he can pass on the evidence of indebtedness in which he has placed his savings. He would have the same attitude toward the farm mortgage if this were offered to him as a standard security instead of a small loan made on minute security to a stranger.

Farm-mortgage banking in the United States has been attempted in the past with disastrous results. During the eighties, the rapid development of the western portion of the Corn Belt encouraged many brokers to market the bonds of such companies, secured by Western farm mortgages. A succession of crop failures throughout this region ruined many of these companies. The failure of the Lombard Investment Company, for example, inflicted heavy losses upon the Eastern investors. Mortgage banking, from these unfortunate experiences, fell into serious discredit, and it is only recently that interest in the subject has revived. It is to be hoped, in the interest of the nation's prosperity, and in order to place sound securities within the investor's reach, that this institution which has been perfected in Europe shall be speedily introduced into the United States.

XVIII

INDUSTRIAL BONDS AND RAILROAD BONDS COMPARED

By industrial bonds we understand the bonds of manufacturing companies, corporations producing iron, steel, machinery of various kinds, textiles, refined sugar, etc. We exclude from the classification of industrial bonds the bonds of mining companies, and the bonds of so-called public service corporations which supply gas, water, light, and transportation to municipalities.

The investor must exercise great caution in purchasing industrial bonds. These bonds are attractive in that they usually pay 5½ and 6 per cent. interest, and can frequently be purchased at prices sufficiently below par to add considerably to this yield. Their security, however, is, as a class, by no means so good as the security of the other classes of bonds which we have investigated.

The bond-buyer, it should be remembered, surrenders a chance of participating in the increasing earnings of the company in exchange for a guarantee of a fixed rate of return on his investment.

INDUSTRIAL BONDS COMPARED

If this guarantee is in any way doubtful, the low price and the high interest return at which the bonds can be purchased will usually be found to be insufficient insurance against the risks of loss. Manufacturing companies, as a rule, cannot give these satisfactory guarantees of security.

The causes of this inferiority of security can be best understood by comparing manufacturing industry, from the standpoint of permanence of the income out of which the interest on the bonds must be paid, with that industry upon which most of the securities of the United States are based—the business of railway transportation. The bonds of manufacturing companies are inferior to railway bonds for the following reasons:

First: The demand for any manufactured product is less stable than the demand for railway transportation in the same territory.

Second: Manufacturing companies are more exposed to competition than railway companies.

Third: The location of manufacturing industry is more liable to frequent changes.

Fourth: The personal equation enters more largely into the management of manufacturing companies than into railway management.

Fifth: Manufacturing industry is more complex, less visible, and, therefore, less easily understood by the investor than the business of railway transportation.

Let us take these points up in order. The demand for the products of a single industry, such as steel, is limited to a small portion of the total number of commodities produced. There are a thousand articles clamoring for the money of the consumer. At best each commodity can absorb only a portion of the demand. The demand for railway transportation, on the other hand, is represented by every commodity of commerce. It corresponds very closely to the entire supply of commodities produced. What is wanted in the earnings of a company to make its bonds secure is stability. Wide fluctuations in earnings, which bring them down close to the limit of fixed charges, always impair the security of the bonds. It is an acknowledged principle of trade that the broader the demand for the products of services of an industry, the more stable are its earnings. This principle is based upon the observation that a large and diversified demand is but slightly affected by any single influence, while if this influence is left to operate by itself upon the price of a commodity or service, it produces wide fluctuations. The withdrawal of 10,000 gallons from a stand-pipe appreciably affects the level of water in the pipe. If the same amount is withdrawn from the reservoir, however, there is no visible change. This illustration may be used to explain the instability of the demand for railway transportation as compared with the demand for coal, sugar, or steel. The railroad company is patronized by the producers of every commodity. What it loses in freight earnings from a decline in price or supply of one group of products, it often more than regains by advances in others.

The manufacturing company, on the other hand, producing, at the most, only a small number of products, has no such compensation for a falling-off in demand. It cannot turn its plant to producing something else. The steel plant, for example, cannot turn to sugar, or the cotton mill to the production of shoes. A railroad, however, can turn from the transportation of hard coal to the transportation of soft coal, or from the transportation of grain to the transportation of manufactured goods, or from carrying iron ore to carrying sand, stone, and cement. It has a thousand uses for its plant, while the manufacturing company has only one. The classi-

14   209

fied freight traffic of the Pennsylvania Railroad, for example, contains 36 general classes of freight, some of which comprise thousands of individual articles, and all of which, taken together, make up the 143,928,382 tons hauled by the Pennsylvania Railroad in 1912. Each one of the manufactured commodities which the Pennsylvania Railroad carries is produced by some industrial concern. Each one of these commodities is acted upon by a variety of influences which affect its supply and demand, and through these increase or diminish the profits of the business which produces it.

The production of anthracite coal, for example, is reduced by a strike. As a result, the demand for bituminous coal is increased. A failure of the corn-crop reduces the profits of the farmer and stock-raiser. A reduction of the tariff lessens the profits of the sugar-refiner, and a reduction of the internal revenue duty on manufactured tobacco increases the profits of the tobacco trust. Profits and prices are in a state of constant change. No manufacturing industry can be certain of its earnings a year hence.

But from these perturbations of commerce, the railway company is, to a large extent, protected.

The immense variety of its traffic prevents rapid changes in the gross amount. What is lost on one commodity is often regained on another, and the total tonnage is not reduced. The experience of the Pennsylvania Railroad, during the anthracite strike of 1902, is in point. This road hauls both anthracite and bituminous coal. As a result of the strike, the anthracite traffic was cut off, and the anthracite railroads, such as the Reading and the Lehigh Valley, suffered a heavy loss. But the Pennsylvania hauled a large part of the bituminous coal which took the place of anthracite in the Eastern markets, and the increased earnings from this source more than offset the loss on anthracite coal.

Manufacturing industry shows no such tendencies toward stability. On the contrary, manufacturing industry is growing constantly more specialized. In place of producing all kinds of shoes, for example, the shoe-manufacturer comes to specialize in women's and children's shoes, and then in women's shoes alone. A manufacturer of machine tools, as the demand for his product increases, will gradually concentrate his production upon lathes, and eventually he may concentrate on a single type of lathe for specialized work.

Large advances in specialization increase the liability to wide fluctuations in demand, corresponding changes in profits, and resulting instability of security.

Manufacturing industry is more exposed to competition than the railroad. A railroad company has a natural monopoly. After the territory through which its line passes has been fully settled, and the day of state and local donations of land and cash has passed away, competition becomes very difficult. More especially is this true because of the increasing expense of terminals in large cities. The Baltimore and Ohio was forced into bankruptcy in 1896, among other causes, by the cost of its entrance into Philadelphia, where it hoped to compete with the Pennsylvania; and the Gould interests, after spending $30,000,000 in an attempt to gain a foothold in Pittsburgh, have been practically forced from the field of competition in that city. Even where railway competition exists between the larger cities, the local traffic is generally free from its influence. Moreover, the way and structure of a railroad may be considered as a permanent plant to which the company is constantly adding. Railway equipment changes very slowly, and no faster than it is worn-out. A well managed manufacturing concern, on the other hand, is constantly throwing into the scrap pile valuable machinery which has been supplanted by some new invention, which must be installed in order to meet competition.

As a railroad grows, the value of its property is constantly being added to, and the cost of duplicating it increases to a point which renders it almost immune from the danger of competition.

Manufacturing industry is seldom free from competition. Even the United States Steel Corporation, with all its advantages, has been unable to retain the control of the market of the steel trade in the United States with which it started. Its percentage of the total production has gone steadily down. Now that the Sherman law is being so effectively enforced, the possibility of monopoly in manufacturing industry may be considered even more remote, since the combinations by which the monopolies of the past have been built up are put under the ban.

Even the patent monopoly is subject to such conditions and limitations as to render it of little value in furnishing security for bond-issues. A patent expires at the end of seventeen years.

The originality of the invention must be tested in court before the patentee can be certain of legal protection in his right. If the invention proves valuable, there are always men or corporations who will attack its originality in the hope of either invalidating the invention in whole or in part, or of receiving money to withdraw their claim. A recent illustration is the invention of the Taylor-White process for the manufacture of tool steel, from which the owners for a number of years drew a large income, but which was finally declared to be non-patentable. It is next to impossible, in this day of accumulated knowledge, to hit upon something which is absolutely new. Somewhere in the world, it may be in an obscure laboratory, or in a corner of some workshop, the most promising invention has been at least suggested, and a suggestion of anticipation is enough for a contest.

The value of a patent, moreover, is constantly threatened by the danger of substitution. The end desired may be reached by some other road than the one upon which the patentee has the exclusive right to travel. As soon as the value of a patent is proved, men set to work upon the problem which it has solved in the endeavor to find some other solution, and it is but seldom that one of them does not succeed. The writer knows of a case where a patent was granted for an improvement in a certain device, in which the only change was the substitution of a weak for a strong spring. As a basis for the security of investment, a patent is worthless. No well informed investor should, save in the most exceptional cases, buy a bond of a company whose earnings are dependent on the monopoly of a patent.

Even those manufacturing industries which rely upon the monopoly of their control of raw material are not secure. It was supposed, for a number of years, that the United States Steel Corporation had achieved a practical monopoly of the ore supply of the United States. Certainly its control was sufficient to put up the price of iron ore to a point which made it exceedingly difficult for the independents, who were obliged to purchase their ore, to make any money. These high prices of ore, however, stimulated the efforts to uncover any new supplies, and brought into use a large number of low-grade ores found in the Eastern States, which it was not profitable to work at former ore prices. Discoveries and development in the northern coast of the island of Cuba also made enormous additions to the supply of available iron ore. At one mine on Nipe Bay, there is in sight over 500,000,000 tons of ore, which can be laid down along the Atlantic Sea-board at much lower prices than this same grade of steel can be furnished from the Lake Superior mines.

The difficulty of achieving a monopoly of manufacture is but another expression for the liability of manufacturing industry to competition, and competition is always dangerous. It is true that a combination of good sense and good fortune may achieve success, but the danger of failure is always present; and even if success is achieved, its measure may be small. The constant imminence of competition makes the investor cautious about buying the long-time bonds of a manufacturing company. He may buy the stock, offsetting the risk by the higher returns on the investment; but in a bond which pays, at best, only a moderate return, the maximum security is demanded.

The three remaining considerations with which this discussion opened, bearing upon the inferiority of manufacturing bonds as compared with railroad bonds, may be passed briefly in review. The location of manufacturing industry is subject to sudden changes. A large part of the heavy iron and steel trade which was formerly controlled by Pittsburgh, is now passing to the Chicago district, and the Northwest, it is expected, will be served from the plants erected at Duluth. The great textile and boot and shoe industries of New England are in danger of arrested development, due to the steady progress of the sentiment in favor of a strict application of the long and short haul clauses. New England has been able to live and thrive because of the exceedingly low railroad rates which they receive on their raw materials shipped in and on their manufactured products shipped out. If the long and short haul clause is strictly applied, and the railroad prevented from charging the same rate for a long haul as it charges for short distances, the industries of New England must seek new outlets in the foreign trade for the domestic business which will be lost to them by the developments in the West and the South.

The personal equation is far more important in manufacturing industry than in railroading. Take, for example, the immense strides which the Bethlehem Steel Company has been making under the leadership of Charles M. Schwab, whose superior as a steel producer does not exist in the United States. Compared with his achievements, the record of the United States Steel Corporation makes but a sorry showing. In manufacturing, the processes and machinery are so complex, and the necessity for change and improvement is so constant, that the ability of the manager is often the deciding factor in the success of the concern.

Compared with the railroad, this inferiority of manufacturing is especially conspicuous. The operations of a railroad are simple and uniform. They repeat themselves under all conditions and in every section. The appliances of a railroad are also relatively simple, and easy to understand and operate. A locomotive engine is the most complicated machine of a railway, and the mechanism of a locomotive is relatively simple. Railroading has been called an exact science. There is little difficulty in filling vacancies in the most important positions. Railway operation is now largely a matter of uniform routine, coupled with sound judgment in financial management, and tact and diplomacy in conducting negotiations with the public and with the employees. The investor in railway bonds may justly concern himself with the financial management of a property, but he can now be confident that the security of his bonds will seldom be impaired by blunders in the operating or construction departments.

" The final consideration affecting the relative value of railway and industrial bonds, is what may be called the 'comprehensibility' of the two industries. The railroad is visible. The bond-buyer, it may be, rides daily over a portion of its lines. Its equipment and its operations are always in evidence. He can see the property and can understand its workings. This character of simplicity extends even to its reports. A properly kept railway report, to a man of average intelligence in such matters, is plain reading. The operations of a railway company consist in transporting a certain number of tons of freight and a certain number of passengers, for a certain amount of money. Its expenses are easily understood. Its equipment can be enumerated in detail. The investor can follow its history from one year to another, and is not obliged to employ an expert to explain its reports to him."

"But the manufacturing company has none of these advantages. Its plant is largely visible. A holder of United States Steel bonds might obtain permission to go through one of the plants, but he would run some risk in doing so. His clothing would be burned into holes by flying sparks. He would have to dodge locomotive engines running at top speed around corners. He would be almost deafened by the noise, and often scorched by the heat. Moreover, for all his pains, he would understand very little of what he saw, and he would not care to repeat the experience. The full report of such a company would be equally unintelligible to the initiated. What does he know about a universal plate mill, or a Wellman-Seaver charging machine, or a Jones mixer? Probably nothing. He has never seen these important appliances of a steel-mill, probably never will see them, and would understand little about them if he should see them. The technical jargon of an engineer's report would be equally unintelligible. An inventor who purchases industrial bonds buys into a company of whose equipment and operations he usually understands very little. I would not be understood to condemn the entire class of industrial bonds.

INDUSTRIAL BONDS COMPARED

There are to be found bonds of manufacturing industries, especially those issued under the serial plan, where the principal is rapidly extinguished out of earnings which are reasonably secure. The high yield of these bonds is also attractive. There is no reason, however, why any one should buy an industrial bond to yield less than 6 per cent., even upon the soundest recommendations and after the most careful investigation; and six per cent. with much better security, can be obtained from a great variety of investments."[1]

---

[1] Quoted from the author's Trust Finance.

XIX

TIMBER BONDS

TEN years ago any first-class banking house in the United States would have immediately rejected a proposition to buy three or five million dollars of bonds secured by a first mortgage on standing timber. Such an undertaking would have been looked upon as too hazardous. The investor could not have been persuaded to put his money into such securities.

Of late years, however, with the steady advance in the cost of living, and the resulting insistent demand for a higher rate of return on investments, combined with the rapid development of financial technique in investigating opportunities for investment, and in formulating plans of capitalization and financial management, standing timber is becoming the basis of bonds which fully deserve the title of investment securities.

The basis of the security in timber bonds is the steadily diminishing timber supply of the United States. The consumption of lumber per capita in this country is rapidly increasing. From 1880 to

1900, the increase in population was 52 per cent. and the increase in the lumber cut was 94 per cent. In 1880, 18,000,000,000 feet of timber was cut in the United States; in 1907, 40,000,000,000 feet. The total amount of standing timber in the United States, including that which is held by the government as forest reserve, as reported by the Bureau of Forestry, is 2,500,000,000,000 feet. This supply is being exhausted at the rate of 100,000,000,000 feet a year, and the prices of all kinds of timber are steadily advancing. The average annual export price of lumber in 1896 reached its lowest figure at $14.56 per thousand feet; in 1911 the price of the same product was $21.55, an increase of 48 per cent. This rapid increase of price is an indication of the fact that at the present rate of cutting, the supply of timber in the United States will be exhausted in from 20 to 25 years. The holders of timber land in this country possess one of the strongest natural monopolies, a monopoly whose value is certain to increase even over the present extraordinary figure.

The successful efforts of the lumber interests to raise large amounts of capital by the sale of bonds have been prompted by the change in the organization of the industry. Until recent years, the logging and milling of timber were carried on by two sets of producers. An accurate picture of the old days in the lumber industry is given in Stewart Edward White's "The Riverman." The logging firms were the owners of timber land and cut out a supply of logs each winter. These logs they would float down the river to the mills where they would be sold. Prices of timber land were low and payments were easy. Only a small amount of capital was required.

This situation has now entirely changed. All branches of the industry are concentrated under a single ownership. One company owns its own timber lands, does its own logging and milling, and in some cases sells its own product. The amount of capital required to operate a business of this character is very large. In the first place, the timber holdings must be large to warrant the construction of a modern mill, which is a costly affair, and to supply it with material for an extended period of years. The logging equipment now includes complete steam railways. The logging and the expense of getting out the logs is much greater. With the rise in the price of timber land, an enormous amount of money is tied up for a long term of years, to be collected only in small amounts as the trees are cut. The lumber operator is obliged to extend credit for periods up to six months. His taxes are constantly increasing, and he must meet his freight-bills and pay-rolls promptly.

Few persons who are not conversant with lumber investments are familiar with the extent of the operations of some of these lumber companies. For example, one of the Southern lumber companies owns 550,000 acres of cypress and yellow pine, containing 3,400,000,000 feet of timber, in Georgia and South Carolina. This company has a net working capital of more than $950,000. Its seven mills and their equipment are valued at $1,250,000. In 1912 the output of this company was 140,000,000 feet. Another company, operating in the far West, owns 70,000 acres of virgin timber lands in Western Oregon, which are estimated to contain over 4,300,000,000 feet of fir, cedar, and other timber. The manufacturing plant of this company is valued at $200,000 and has a capacity of 150,000 feet for each ten-hour day.

In recent years it has been found impossible by the lumber companies to handle their rapidly growing business with the capital derived from their own operations. The investment-banker has, therefore, been appealed to, to furnish funds. The result has been the issuance of a type of bond which combines high-grade security with high interest. One bond-house in Chicago, which has specialized on this type of security, has already sold over $40,000,000 of timber bonds.

Timber bonds are peculiar among industrial securities in that they are issued against property which already exists and which can be accurately measured. A bond issued on the security of rail-road property depends upon the continued profitable operation of the railroad. A rate war, or a change in management, or a long-continued industrial depression, may reduce net earnings below the level of fixed charges. No matter how costly the property of the railroad, the corporation may be forced into bankruptcy, and the bond-holders suffer loss. The farm mortgage depends for its security upon the regular and profitable operation of the farm. Bonds issued on the security of minerals, with the possible exception of anthracite-coal bonds, are likely to be disturbed by the discovery of new supplies of the same mineral.

TIMBER BONDS

The supply of timber, however, is known and fixed. The trees can actually be measured and counted. Their value is known, and that value is steadily increasing. All that is required, therefore, to make these bonds a safe investment, is that they should be issued by an established company in high credit and managed by experienced lumber men; that the lands should contain a known amount of timber of good quality, the exact amount to be ascertained by timber estimators employed by the banking house; that the titles to the land should be found perfect; and that the mortgage securing the bonds should contain provisions which will provide for the repayment of a certain amount of the principal at fixed intervals, so that, before the timber is exhausted, the bonds will have been paid.

How carefully these requirements are complied with, in the issuing of timber bonds, may be seen from a recent bond offering by an important Boston house. The amount of the issue in this case was $6,000,000 of 6 per cent. bonds. These bonds begin to mature in July, 1914, and are finally paid off in serial instalments on July 1, 1922, the instalments rising from $250,000 to $375,000. This is an example of the well known plan of serial bond issues. The property of the company is valued at $16,800,000, or 2.8 times this issue. Provision for the repayment of the bonds is made by a sinking fund, which places in the hands of the trustees, for every thousand feet cut by the company's mills, $3.50. Before the first instalment falls due, the accumulation in the sinking fund will amount to $250,000. As a result of the operation of this sinking fund, the margin of security for the investor is steadily increasing. At the outside, the bonds will represent $1.76 per thousand feet of standing timber. This will be reduced, by the operation of the sinking fund, to $1.40 per thousand feet on January 1, 1917, to 89 cents per thousand feet on July 1, 1919, and to 27 cents per thousand feet of standing timber on July 1, 1921.

This company operates in a district which has never been disturbed or seriously damaged by fire. The mortgage securing the bonds provides that the saw-mills and manufactured lumber shall be fully protected by fire insurance. The Company has been in successful operation for 40 years. It is managed by men experienced in timber investment and saw-mill operations, who own practically the entire capital stock of the company. The proceeds of the issue are employed for additional working capital and to increase the timber reserves. The net earnings of the company for the present year are estimated at $1,000,000, as compared with the interest requirement on the bonds of $360,000.

These statements are made by the banking house on the basis of a careful investigation. The bankers themselves verify the statements made on behalf of the management as to the history of the company, and the standing of those in control of it. For the financial results of the operation, the bankers rely upon the examination of chartered accountants. The report of these accountants they submit in connection with the offering of the bonds. In this case, the accountants' report showed that the average manufacturing profits for the past 6 years have been $5.81 per thousand feet of lumber sold.

The most important investigation made on behalf of the bankers is the amount of standing timber. This report is signed by Mr. W. E. Straight, one of the leading timber experts in the United States, whose name on a report is positive proof of a thorough preliminary examination. The method employed by Mr. Straight is

described in a booklet issued by Messrs. Clark L.
Poole & Co. of Chicago, one of the leading banking houses in this line, in part as follows:

All corners having been established, Mr. Straight assigned
the crews to work. They were started at different points and
worked to a common centre, with the intention to have all the
crews meet about the same time. Each crew is furnished with
plans of the different portions of the land allotted to it, the
descriptions all being checked from the original deeds to the
property. . . . A camp will be occupied on an average of
about ten days; and the crews will cover from 10 to 17 sections
of land from one camp, depending on the character of the country.

Each crew covers on foot the several portions of the woods
assigned to it. The crew starts at some point on the base given
by the surveyor and continues to do its work, keeping an accurate
check on its base as the work proceeds. The method used is
known as "horse-shoeing a 40," and is the one most commonly
used by Mr. Straight, as it enables the cruiser to see every portion of the land. If the start is made at the southeast corner of
a section, the cruiser will say to his compassman: "Go to tally
1 north." When the compassman, who runs all the lines, has
gone north 125 paces, or about 375 feet he calls out: "Tally 1
north," and stops until he is directed to move. This gives one
side of a ten-acre tract.

The cruiser has begun to work toward the compassman, and
counts and estimates each and every tree for a distance of 25
paces on each side of his base line, making 50 paces in all. At
first he measures the trees with a tape, to verify his eye judgment
of the circumference and measures windfalls for length to verify
his eye judgment as to the height of trees. If his eye judgment
has been at fault, he keeps measuring until his eye judgment
becomes accurate, then he trusts solely to his eye. He keeps
tally of each tree, and at the close of the day figures out his totals
by an established mathematical rule. . . . When the esti-

mator has finished his work . . . he has an accurate tally of each tree on eight acres of each 40 acres, with its length and other dimensions. In his hand he has held a card on which he has kept a tally. He also carries a field book in which he notes the topography of the land, the location of marshes, lakes, streams, wagon loads, logging railroads, and everything that comes within his observation, together with notations as to the surface of the ground, general logging chance, character of soil, etc. At night he makes out from his field book an accurate plat, or timber section and field report sheet, one for each section of land estimated.

It is on the basis of carefully detailed work of this sort, carried on under the direct supervision of the supervisor, that the banking house estimates the quantity of timber on which it advances money. When this estimate is supplemented by a verification of details, and by the drawing of a trust deed conveying the timber and all other property of the company, in trust for the payment of principal and interest of the bonds, under a variety of carefully drawn restrictions which practically eliminate the risk of careless financial management, the banking house can offer the investor a 6 per cent. bond which is as safe an investment as can be furnished him.

XX

INDUSTRIAL PREFERRED STOCK

EVERY part of the United States is the seat of old and prosperous manufacturing enterprises, many of them dating back to the middle of the last century, with long records of solvency and profit. Fifteen years ago, when the industrial trust movement started, a large number of these concerns were swept into consolidations, and their owners seized the opportunity to retire. This industrial trust movement, however, was aimed not at the investor, but at the speculator. The stocks of these much-criticised combinations were not sold by investment-bankers to their clients, but were marketed on the public stock-exchanges by the methods of public advertising and manipulation. For a long time the investor would have nothing to do with them.

Following the collapse of the consolidation movement, about 1903, the flotation of industrial preferred stocks languished, and not until the last three years has this class of securities seriously engaged the attention of the financial world.

INDUSTRIAL PREFERRED STOCK

This time it is not the speculative promoter who creates the new issue, but the investment-banker, anxious to satisfy the insistent demands of his clients for a security which will furnish them reasonable safety with a higher rate of return than they can secure from the purchase of bonds. The result has been a large number of preferred stock issues covering every kind of business. Agricultural machinery companies, canning companies, biscuit companies, clothing companies, automobile and trading companies, have all contributed to supply the now enormous total of these industrial preferred stocks.

The usual investigations are made by the banker in marketing these securities. If he is conscientious, however, he does not recommend them in the same unqualified terms as those which he employs in advocating the purchase of a mortgage bond. The policy of one very large house is to discourage the sale of preferred stocks to the small investor. It recognizes that there is an element of speculation in these securities. They must be classified as speculative investments. There are few manufacturing enterprises which are sufficiently prosperous to guarantee seven per cent. to the investor in good times and bad. Those who purchase these securities must take the risk of business depression, from which the holders of well selected bonds are now nearly immune.

The banker does his best to protect his client who buys preferred stock, by inserting in the contract, under which the preferred stock is issued, a variety of restrictions, all of which are calculated to secure the investor. Preferred stocks are now universally made cumulative as to dividends, and also as to assets. By this provision, in case a period of depression should force the management to pass the dividend for one year, this unpaid dividend must be made up before the common stock-holders can receive anything. There is also a preference as to assets in the event of liquidation. In the unlikely event that the company should desire to dissolve, realize on its property, and distribute the proceeds, the preferred stock-holder would be paid first.

An effort is made, also, to enforce conservative financial management upon the company. It is almost universally provided that no mortgage can be placed upon any of the property held by the company without the consent of the holders of three-fourths of the preferred stock. In some cases the company is prohibited from issuing bonds of any kind, whether secured by mortgage or not, which would rank ahead of the preferred stock, maturing more than one year from the date of issue. Some restrictions require the company to set aside a sinking fund out of earnings before any dividends are paid on the common stock, and to retire a certain portion of the preferred stock each year. Again, it is frequently provided that the quick assets—cash, good accounts receivable, materials and supplies, and half finished and finished products of the company—must at all times equal the amount of preferred stock outstanding.

If these requirements are not carried out by the directors, in addition to the penalty of a prohibition on common stock dividends, it is sometimes provided that the exclusive voting power shall vest in the preferred stock-holders, who are placed in control of the company until the provisions of the contract have been complied with. These restrictions are excellent. They are calculated to secure the investor. They cannot, however, impart to preferred stock the security of a mortgage bond, secured not only by earnings but by properties specifically set aside for its protection.

Even with all these safeguards and restrictions, preferred stock ranks after all forms of indebtedness. Its dividends are payable only when earned, and then at the discretion of the directors. It ranks ahead of common stock, it is true, but during periods of depression, or in case the directors pursue an unwise policy, involving the company in financial embarrassment, the holders of the preferred stock must be prepared to stand the loss. They must recognize that they are not creditors of the company, but merely owners; that in any final adjustment or liquidation of the company's affairs the creditors' claims must first be satisfied, and the preferred stock-holders must take what is left.

A melancholy example of misfortune of this character is furnished by the fate of the McCrum-Howell Company, a corporation engaged in the manufacture of radiators, boilers, and enameled ware, which in 1910 made a large issue of preferred stock for the purpose of acquiring control of companies manufacturing vacuum-cleaners and other appliances.

I have before me the circular issued by the

236

fiscal agents under date of November 1, 1910, and containing a variety of information which was then believed to be accurate, but which subsequent events proved was not correct. The assets of the company amounted to $7,425,685, according to this statement. Against these assets, there was no debt. The liabilities included $3,500,000 of common stock and an equal amount of cumulative preferred stock, a surplus of $333,-185 and a reserve of $92,500. The charter of the company provided that no bonds could be placed upon the property of the company except with the consent of the total outstanding stock. The proceeds from the sale of this preferred stock increased the net working capital of the company to $2,408,597, which, it was stated, "provides the company with ample working capital to care for its increasing business." The accounts of the several companies, it is stated on the authority of "chartered accountants," show net earnings of $640,195, over two and one-half times the dividend requirements on the entire issue of preferred stock. Dividends of 3 per cent. were being paid on the common stock. As a result of the consolidation, large increases in earnings were expected.

One of the banker's circulars concluded as follows:

THE CAREFUL INVESTOR

From the standpoint of security, stability of earnings, liberal income return, marketability, and promise of appreciation in value, we regard the above stock as a safe and attractive investment. Our recommendation is based on our own intimate knowledge of the affairs of the company for the past five years.

This issue was offered by a number of banking houses to their clients. It is presumed that they made proper investigations into the affairs of the various companies, and that they had confidence in the merits of the scheme. Certainly the issue, although not as good as some others, was, on the face of these statements, of a very good quality. The new company had no debts. Its earnings were equal to two and one-half times the preferred dividend requirements. With a prospect of large increases in those earnings, the investor could be reasonably certain that his preferred dividends would be regularly paid, or that, in case it proved necessary to suspend these dividends, he would risk nothing more than a postponement of his income. This was on November 1, 1910.

Sixteen months later we find the following news item:

Justice Buffington, in the United States District Court at Philadelphia, appointed Edward R. Stettinius, President of the Diamond Match Co., and Walter D. Updegraff, of Philadelphia, receivers, on application of A. F. Pfahler of Philadelphia, who, it is said, owns $310,300 stock. The company agreed to the receivership, but declared that inability to realize on assets, and not insolvency, was the cause of its troubles.

The bill alleges that the company is perfectly solvent, but that a reorganization is necessary; that the company has suffered extremely in the last six months from a sudden contraction in trade, due in great measure to the Government's suit against the "bathtub trust," which also hurt the company's credit. There is said to be outstanding about $1,800,000 in commercial paper in the hands of many parties, maturing within the next four months, of which $300,000 matures before March 31, and "quick" assets in excess of commercial paper which cannot be turned into money to meet obligations. The liabilities are stated to aggregate $2,118,000, and the quick assets $1,749,000, consisting of accounts receivable, $1,480,000; bills receivable, $219,000, and cash, $50,000.

On September 27th we have another news item—the report of the receivers. In place of temporary embarrassment, we now find revealed a condition of absolute bankruptcy. Mr. Albert H. Wiggin, Chairman of the Creditors' Committee, says in substance: "Our investigations have convinced us that if the property be disposed of at a forced sale, the creditors can realize but a small percentage of their claims. The business, however, appears to have an earning power. Mr. Strong estimates the earnings, after making certain improvements, at $209,000 a year, with a gradual increase. Others name higher figures."

The receivers presented at this time a statement of assets, in place of the $7,425,685 set forth in the letter of the president of the company, "submitted and verified by the Safeguard Account Company, Chartered Public Accountants," to the amount of $2,179,361, a shrinkage of $5,200,000 in two years and three months. The liabilities of the company, which were so clear and clean two years before, now present a melancholy spectacle. They include accounts payable, $326,-647; bills payable, $2,047,053; endorsed or guaranteed paper, $212,693; a total of $2,586,394. And in addition there were over $700,000 of unproved claims. The receivers further say: "The company originally manufactured boilers, radiators, enameled bath-tubs, lavatories, 'etc., but early in 1910 adopted a policy of expansion, to which its embarrassment is largely attributable. None of these purchases proved profitable; the portable vacuum-cleaner business resulted in heavy losses."

One last news item completes the story.

Justice Buffington in the United States District Court in Philadelphia, on November 13, 1912, affirmed the sale of the assets and property of the company, to a committee representing the creditors, for $870,000 cash. The offer was made two weeks ago, over 80 per cent. of the creditors having consented thereto. The reorganization will be effected at once.

I do not claim that this disaster which eliminated $3,500,000 of preferred stock, into which large investors had put their money, and destroyed a large common stock equity, is typical of what will befall other industrial corporations which have put out their securities on the strength of banker's recommendations and seven per cent. dividends. This case is, no doubt, exceptional. It does, however, show how quickly the aspect of prosperity may be changed by unwise financial management, and especially by a rapid increase in debt. The preferred stock-holder is powerless to prevent such a catastrophe. Even though his contract with the company prohibits the directors from issuing any evidences of debt maturing in more than one year, they cannot be restricted in making bank loans or in buying merchandise on account.

I have before me a list compiled by a large financial institution, of the notes and paper of various industrial corporations outstanding at various dates in 1911 and 1912. The totals in some cases are very large and are rapidly increasing. These floating debts represent a constant menace to the solvency of these companies. They carry a threat of receivership and foreclosure sale which the stockholder cannot disregard. When the directors, therefore, propose an issue of bonds or notes to fund these floating debts, the stockholders can do nothing less than to consent. To refuse their consent is to invite disaster. What, then, becomes of this much vaunted restriction as to note issues and mortgages? It is valueless in the face of such a situation.

A large corporation, with a record of over sixty years of continuous growth, a little more than a year ago issued $8,000,000 of preferred stock, with the usual restrictions for the protection of the preferred stock-holders. The total accounts and bills payable of this company were, in round numbers, $2,700,000, with a surplus of assets over current liabilities of nearly $19,000,000. A few months later this company announced a large issue of notes for the purpose of refunding its floating debt. These notes come ahead of the preferred stock, and there is no way in which the holders of the preferred stock can prevent their issue.

I would not be understood to condemn industrial preferred stocks. They should be characterized as speculative investments. Most of them will, no doubt, continue to pay regular dividends. But such securities should be purchased only from the most reliable banking houses, who will stand back of the issue, and who will not hesitate to use their great power as fiscal agents of the company to prevent unwise and extravagant management, and the departure from lines of policy whose wisdom has been proven by the experience of long success. The purchaser of such stocks must also realize that he is taking a risk; that seven per cent. is not compatible with an assurance of absolute safety, and that in the event of a recurrence of industrial depression he must be prepared to submit to a postponement of his dividends.

XXI

THE DISSOLUTION OF THE TRUSTS

JUDGMENT day for the trusts has arrived. Some of them, we hope, are good, and some of them are evil. The federal courts are now, and will be for a long time, occupied in separating the sheep from the goats. The Supreme Court, in the Oil and Tobacco cases, has set up a standard by which to decide which of these great companies is lawful, and which must be dissolved.

The opinion of the court is clear that any corporation engaged in interstate commerce (which includes all the trusts), and which has been formed not "with the legitimate purpose of reasonably forwarding personal interest and developing trade, but on the contrary were of such a character as to give rise to the inference or presumption that they had been entered into or done with the intent to do wrong to the general public, and to limit the right of individuals, thus restraining the free flow of commerce, and tending to bring about the evils such as enhancement of prices which were considered to be against public policy," is unlawful under the Sherman Act.

The court says, in effect, that any large company or collection of companies, formed with the purpose of limiting competition, that is advancing or keeping up prices, or which, after its promotion, uses its power to limit competition, so that prices can be advanced, is an unlawful organization and must be dissolved. In the light of these decisions the legal position of the large companies formed in the last twenty years, to put together sometimes thirty smaller concerns which had been competing with one another, is very doubtful. Most people who own securities of any kind have the preferred or common stocks of these industrials. There are large companies, all organized on the model of the Standard Oil Company, whose stock prices appear in the daily New York quotations. If the movement against the trusts continues, all these hundreds of thousands of stock-holders—the Steel Trust alone has over 100,000—must adjust themselves to new conditions. Until this adjustment is made, or so long as the fear of it is present, what we call prosperity will not return.

How will this adjustment be made? How can

the trusts be dissolved, in such a manner as the court says, "to protect, not to destroy, rights of property?" A word about the organization of the trusts. Here are five corporations, A, B, C, D, and E, making shoes, or steel, or pumps, or harvesting machinery. These companies are competitors; they are constantly fighting one another—raiding one another's customers; cutting prices, secretly and sometimes openly; making agreements, gentlemen's agreements, and then breaking them; stealing or corrupting one another's employees; biting and clawing each other in the bear-pit of competition; behaving like mediæval captains of brigands instead of modern captains of industry. The men who control these companies decide to combine and so stop the waste of competition.

Suppose, for the sake of simplicity, the stock of each of these five companies is $2,000,000, each share having a face value of $100. A New Jersey corporation is organized, which issues $20,000,000 of stock—$10,000,000 preferred and $10,000,000 common. The preferred stock is entitled to receive $700,000, seven per cent., before anything is paid on the common. The consolidation is now formed by the exchange of one share of preferred stock and one share of common stock of the New Jersey corporation for each of the 100,000 shares of the five companies. The New Jersey company—let us call it the Amalgamated Company—now owns $10,000,000 of the five companies and their former stock-holders own $10,000,000 of the preferred and common stocks, $2.00 for $1.00 of the stock of the five companies—an operation familiar to most people as stock watering.

Immediately price-cutting, misrepresentation, slander, back-biting, everything that goes under the name of cut-throat competition, is at an end between them. The Amalgamated Company is the sole owner of all five, electing directors, choosing officers, establishing prices, driving these five tamed animals to one vehicle and in one set of harness. Every feature of the business policy is now reduced to rule and order. The territory over which, as competitors, all were accustomed to raid and foray, is divided among them. One of the five plants may be out of date, badly located. Its business is divided among the other four. The general administration is centred in New York; financing, buying, advertising supervision, all are managed from a central office. In place of war, concord, peace, and harmony succeed within the circle of these former rivals. The new company may not advance prices, but it gets from the customer those prices which it publishes; every one pays the same prices. There are no rebates, no special discounts, no allowances.

This, in brief, is the change which was accomplished by the organization of the trusts. There is a darker side to the picture. Stories and sworn statements of the wrongful and oppressive use of the great power of these great corporations are numerous. Business, however, is not conducted to the strains of soft melody. At best, some of its practices are not pretty. Probably the two culprits did no more, nor as much, against the moral law, when their enormous size is considered, than the average grocer or milkman. In passing, it may be observed that in the grocery trade, to quote but one instance, there are three prices for the same coffee done up in different packages.

The Supreme Court did not, however, heed these charges. It passed them over. To arrive at the conclusion that the Standard Oil and the American Tobacco Companies should be dissolved, it was not necessary to inquire whether these companies were benevolent despotisms. That they were, or aimed to be, supreme in their respective fields, was sufficient to condemn them, and to condemn any other company which by the consolidation of competitors has reached a position similarly exalted.

Since the Standard Oil Trust has passed out of existence, a word in its favor may be more favorably received than when it was alive. *De mortuis nihil nisi bonum.*

One of the undisclosed abuses in the railway industry is the open violation by many shippers of the classification rules of the railroads. There are five classifications into which falls every commodity save such as are carried on special rates, like coal and lumber. The rates are highest on Class I, and fall to Class V. The basis of distinction between these classes is the cost or risk to the railroad in shipping them, together, in some cases, with the value of the article. An article which is carefully boxed or crated will take a Class III rate, while if it is not protected from breakage, it will take a Class II rate.

There was a liveryman in an Iowa town who needed a carload of horses. Emigrant movables, including furniture and live stock, take a very low rate. The railroads seek to encourage settlement. Horses take a high rate. Our friend was familiar with these facts. He went to Montana, bought his horses, loaded with them into a car two kitchen-chairs, an old stove, and some domestic *bric-à-brac*, and billed the whole as "household movables." Another enterprising shipper also billed the following articles as household movables: portable forge, 2 sinks, 1 bundle rakes, 1 wire gate, 6 loose sledges, 1 barrel lanterns, 2 wheelbarrows, 1 box pipe-fittings, 200 reels of barb wire. These cases are not exceptional. More than a thousand are reported daily in New York City alone. Each offense is punishable by fine or imprisonment, or both, at the discretion of the court.

To detect these misdescriptions, the railroads maintain inspection bureaus, whose inspectors are constantly on the alert to raise the freight on way-bills incorrectly made out. Nothing else is done. Until recently the Interstate Commerce Commission has not been willing to act in the matter. Why should the railroads concern themselves with the enforcement of the law. Chicago is one of the centres of misdescription. The inspectors are constantly on the watch to detect violations of the law and to raise the rates. The list of habitual offenders is long, and contains some honored names; but the name of the Standard Oil Company of Indiana is not among them. An official of one of the inspection bureaus told me that in a service of thirteen years not one of his inspectors had ever reported even a minor infraction of the rules by the Standard Oil Company.

Let us consider another instance of a different kind. When a man or a corporation has something to sell, he or it can usually be relied upon to put a high value upon it. Sometimes, even when the sellers are very conservative, the value is excessive. A large public-service company, owning plants in many cities, recently arranged to purchase a gas company owned by the Standard Oil Company interests, and managed according to Standard Oil methods. In the schedule of assets submitted for the consideration of the buyers appeared this item, "Securities owned, $200,000." The president of the purchasing company pounced instantly upon this. He became suspicious. He resolved to investigate. He had experience with "Securities owned." He knew how worthless they might be. He asked the vendor's attorney for a list of these "securities." The attorney said, "They are all bonds." "Bonds of what?" "United States Government Bonds," was the answer. The gas company had put aside a large amount out of its earnings in the safest securities in the world.

These old-fashioned business virtues of strict obedience to the laws of business, caution in paying out profits, prompt payment of bills, accurate accounting and bookkeeping, avoidance of debt, fair and honorable treatment of employees, maintenance of high standards of product—virtues for which the Standard Oil Company has always been distinguished—are, of course, not to be weighed in the balance against "the intent and purpose to maintain the dominion over the oil industry"; but they are at least not so common even among the critics of the company as to pass unnoticed. Indeed, the possession and recent practice of these virtues by certain men prominent in the magazine field would have saved them control of their properties which have passed into other hands. Let us hope that with the breaking up of the Standard Oil Company there will be a general diffusion of certain of its principles and business methods in quarters which now know them not.

These trusts, by the mandate of the court, are now being dissolved. The method which has been followed in each dissolution is to distribute the assets of the New Jersey companies among their stockholders. Take the case assumed above, for example. The Amalgamated Company has issued 100,000 shares of preferred and 100,000 shares of common stock. It has in its treasury 100,000 shares of the stocks of the five companies. On these stocks it has been collecting dividends and paying out these dividends to its own stockholders. The court now orders this company to dissolve. It adopts the method, so called, of a pro rata distribution of assets. Each of the five companies changes its charter so as to turn 50,000 shares of common stock into 50,000 shares of preferred stock, still in the hands of the New Jersey company, the Amalgamated, the sole owner of all the shares. Then for each share of its preferred stock the Amalgamated gives one-fifth share of the preferred stocks of each of the five companies, and for each share of its common stock it gives one-fifth share of common stock in each of the five companies. The Amalgamated Company can now be dissolved. Its stockholders have all of its assets. For all practical purposes, it has ceased to be. The five original companies remain, but now, instead of their ownership and control being in the hands of the Amalgamated Company, they are owned, it may be, by 1,000 individuals holding from 5 to 1000 shares each. This method with some variations has been applied to dissolve the Oil Trust, the Tobacco Trust, the Powder Trust, and all the rest of the condemned.

Now comes the rub. Cut-throat competition is bad. This is generally recognized. Mr. Andrew Carnegie was the last apostle of the old competitive régime, and he passed out of business ten years ago. For several years Mr. Elbert H. Gary has been conducting a school of coöperation for iron and steel products. His classes have been largely attended, and the lectures have been both interesting and instructive. At the last session of the class in coöperation, held at the Waldorf-Astoria on May 29, 1911, Judge Gary summed up the objects and results of the course as follows:

Whatever we do with reference to prices, whatever we may decide is necessary in order to protect our interests on this occasion and under these circumstances, in my opinion it is highly important for the long future that we continue our relations of friendship and open and frank expression with reference to what we are doing. Now, I do not know the feeling of the rest of you. I do not know what you are disposed to do. I think that so far as we are concerned we would be largely influenced by the action of others, and while insisting upon the position from which I have never varied, I would not, under any circumstances, make any agreement, expressed or implied, direct or indirect, to maintain certain prices, to keep away from customers, to divide territory, to restrict output, or to make any agreement of any sort or description with you or any of you, because, as I understand the law, I have no right to do it; yet at the same time I would do what I have always said I would do; I would tell you and each of you at any time exactly what we are doing; I would give you the names of our customers; I would tell you what prices we were charging; I would give you any information concerning our business, concerning our mills, concerning our clients, concerning ourselves, that you wanted to have, so long as you have the same disposition toward me.

Competition should relate to standards of product, to promptness of delivery, to service, and should not refer to price. Railroads compete furiously for passenger business, yet they do not cut rates. They merely increase the speed and comfort of their trains. Price-cutting in any trade quickly leads to demoralization. It destroys confidence, makes coöperation impossible, leads to deterioration in quality, and makes business uncertain and hazardous. Again, quoting Judge Gary:

There is only a certain amount of business. You can get it away from your friend for a day or a week; perhaps you can make a contract for a time and get a particular order; but in the long run, on the average, month by month, year by year, you cannot get and keep his business.

Granting the evils of competition in prices, and the superiority of coöperative methods in business, the fact remains that the temptation to cut prices in dull times in order to get business from competitors is almost irresistible. The buyer, taking naturally and without effort the rôle of Satan, shows the seller a promised land of profitable contracts, new business, future connections, if only the seller will cut the price. Times are hard, business is slow, debts are pressing. It is almost too much to expect of a man of small calibre that he shall set his face like a flint against the blandishments and alluring inducements of the buyer. And yet, if he yields, the evil spirit of price-competition, accompanied by seven other devils, will return to the house from which the trust movement expelled him, and the last state of American business will be worse than the first.

Here lies the danger to the prosperity of the United States in the dissolution of the trusts. Broken up, as they will be, into a thousand small companies, strictly forbidden to combine, each with its separate officers, its own board of directors, can ruinous competition be prevented? Will these directors and officers be big enough to adhere to the prices published by the leaders in the trade, and, so far as the law allows, will they coöperate for mutual benefit by disclosing to one another their lists of customers and the terms on which they do business? If the American business man can rise to the emergency presented by the dissolution of the trusts, the decisions will prove to have been of great benefit.

For there is another side to the trust picture, a side which is by no means attractive. Large aggregations of widely scattered plants, managed by hired men, supervised by directors who represent thousands of stock-holders with no other interest in the industry than to get their dividends, cannot be managed with the same energy, efficiency, and economy as smaller industrial units can be handled. The cost of production of the trusts, speaking broadly, is far above the cost of the best plants which went into the trusts, although it is lower than that of the poorest plants. An intelligent, energetic group of partners or stock-holders, with ample capital, operating a single plant, can produce at lower cost than can a large and scattered aggregation of plants managed by hired men, no matter how intelligent and conscientious.

In conversation recently upon the subject of centralized management, a well known engineer cited his own experience in managing a group of public-service corporations from a New York office. Daily reports were forwarded to him from each company, and he was in instant touch with every emergency. He found, however, after a series of costly experiments, that the plan would not work. Mistakes would occur which he would correct, but the mistakes could not be anticipated or the resulting losses prevented. He was eventually compelled to abandon the system of centralized management, and place each company upon its own footing, with its own responsible head.

In so far as the trusts are concerned, it is a simple matter to prove that these "economies of combination" are largely imaginary. It will be recalled that, in organizing our hypothetical combination, preferred stock in the Amalgamated Company was given share for share to the stockholders of the five companies that went into the combination, and also an equal amount of common stock. This common stock, in most cases, was "water"; that is to say, it did not represent any value in existence. It was supposed to represent the "economies of combination." Each of the five plants was worth $2,000,000 before the trust was formed. By putting them together, destroying competition among them, reducing unnecessary expenses, and with the advantages of high-grade management, this value, it was assumed, would be increased to $4,000,000, or the value of the five from $10,000,000 to $20,000,-000. This plan was followed in nearly every case.

Now, if we wish to discover the value and extent of these "economies," it is only necessary to look at the quotations of these common stocks. Most of the trusts have been in existence eight years or more, and the period of their life includes some of the most profitable years in the history of American industry. They have had plenty of time to realize these economies. If there is a basis for the organization of consolidations of numerous plants, managed by a board of directors in New York, the common stocks, which represent the "economies of combination"—the savings from buying in large quantities, the lower rates of interest paid to the banks, the superior talents of high salaried men, along with the admitted gains from stable prices—would appear in high dividends and high prices for the stocks.

And yet we find such quotations as these, representing the percentage of $100 per share, at which the trust common stocks are now selling: Allis Chalmers, 9½; American Beet Sugar, 39¾; American Agricultural Chemical, 46; American Can 8⅞; American Car and Foundry 50¼; American Locomotive, 35¾; and so on.   There are a few exceptions, but for the most part, so far as the market quotations of the trust stocks are concerned, the "economies of combination" do not exist.   It is possible that the United States has paid too high a price in an industrial development arrested by the stagnant routine of monopoly for the benefits of suppressed competition.

XXII

THE INVESTOR AND GOLD SUPPLY

In a series of articles recently published in *Cotton and Finance*, dealing with the subject of gold production and its effect upon the prices of bonds, stocks, and commodities, Mr. Theodore H. Price reaches a conclusion which, if it can be established, is of vital moment to every owner of property in the United States, whether that property be bonds, insurance policies, stocks, or real estate. This conclusion, briefly stated, is that the increasing production of gold is responsible for the great rise of prices which has been the characteristic feature of the last decade; that this increased production of gold will continue indefinitely; and that the world is facing an economic crisis arising out of the certainty of a persistent depreciation in its standard of value.

This subject has been much discussed in recent years, as the steady rise of prices has brought home to every class in the community the importance of the problem presented. The fact of the advance of prices is well established. In 1896

Bradstreet's compilation of the wholesale prices of 106 commodities, including all the leading commodities of commerce, was 59,124. In 1900, this figure had risen to 78,839; in 1905, to 80,987; and in 1912, to 90,362. Specimen increases in particular commodities are even more striking. For example, the price of wheat, during this period of seventeen years, rose from 64 cents to $1.22; the price of corn, from 33 cents to 86 cents; the price of beef cattle, from 4.6 cents to 9 cents; eggs, from 12 cents to 20 cents; raw cotton from 7 cents to 11 cents; anthracite coal from $4.25 to $5.50; and so on, with hardly any exception, throughout the entire list. This rise of prices is mainly responsible for the high cost of living. The advance of prices is lessening the purchasing power of gold over the necessaries of life.

The competition of corporations for the money of the investor, on the other hand, because of the rapid multiplication of companies, and the numerous safeguards which its experience and information is teaching the bankers to throw about the stocks and bonds which they offer for sale, is growing constantly sharper, and is forcing down the prices of all securities which carry a fixed income, and which have no prospect of sharing in increasing profits. The investment fund, it is true, is steadily increasing, but since the purchasing power of a 4 per cent. or 5 per cent. investment income is so rapidly declining, while, at the same time, the number of securities offering these rates of interest is increasing, the natural result is that the investor discriminates against so-called "gilt-edge" bonds. This depreciation in the prices of bonds, while apparently it is an advantage to investors making new purchases, is threatening heavy losses to the owners of investments already in existence.

Few realize to what an enormous total the securities of bonds and stocks issued by American corporations has mounted. In an article by Francis Lynde Stetson, published in the *Atlantic Monthly* for July, 1912, which is quoted by Mr. Price, the following statement is made:

In the fiscal year 1909, according to the report of the Commissioner of Internal Revenue, there were in the United States 262,490 corporations of all kinds, with more than $84,000,000,000 of stocks and bonds, and $3,125,000,000 of income, paying a Federal tax of about $27,000,000. For the fiscal year 1910–11 the figures had risen to 270,000 corporations, with more than $88,000,000,000 of stock and bonds, and $3,360,000,000 of income, paying a federal tax of $29,432,000. As the total wealth of the United States has been estimated at $125,000,000,000, it would appear that nearly two-thirds of it is held by corporations.

THE CAREFUL INVESTOR

Approximately one-third of this immense mass of securities represents promises to pay gold at various dates in the future, and the value of the commodity which these bonds promise to pay is falling with every advance in the average price of other commodities. Standard railroad bonds which, fifteen years ago, were selling on a 3½ per cent. basis, have now fallen in price until they yield between 4¼ and 4¾ per cent., and their decline is persistent. During the past year, the decline in the prices of all kinds of bonds has been noteworthy. Every variety of bonds—railroad, industrial, municipal—has suffered from the depreciation of investments.

On the other hand, this same period which has witnessed such a marked decline in the value of bonds has shown an even more pronounced advance in the prices of stocks. The average price of 36 standard railroad and industrial stocks in 1896 was $62.50; in May, 1912, this average price had almost doubled, rising to $118. The reason is as follows: A share of stock represents a right to participate in the distribution of profits of the corporation. These profits tend to increase during periods of rising prices, because the costs of production and distribution, including a large amount of fixed expense, as, for example, interest, depreciation, etc., do not advance to correspond with the increase in the selling value of the product. Every business which depends upon the sale of a commodity has felt the stimulating influence of rising prices. Even the public-service corporations, whose prices and rates are fixed by law and custom—the railroads, street-railways, gas, electric light, and water companies—have profited enormously from the immense business which the advance of prices has so greatly assisted to produce. It is no wonder, therefore, that the prices of the stocks which promised their holders participation in this recent flood of industrial profits should have scored such rapid advances.

Here, then, is the situation. The advance of prices shows no sign of stopping. With every increase in commodity prices, the purchasing power of gold declines. Every form of corporate debt, every variety of bonds, is a promise to pay this commodity which is so rapidly depreciating in value. Of necessity, therefore, prices of bonds decline as the prices of commodities advance. On the other hand, rising prices mean rising profits, and the prices of stocks which participate in those rising profits advance far more rapidly than bonds decline.

The conclusion is inevitable, and Mr. Price has no hesitation in emphasizing it in the strongest possible terms. If the advance of prices is to continue, the investor should discriminate against all bonds, mortgages, and notes which are simply contracts to deliver at a future date so many grains of gold, since the purchasing power of that gold is constantly diminishing, and should prefer agricultural, timber, and mineral lands, and corporation stocks. In other words, if the depreciation of gold is to continue, the prices of bonds must persistently depreciate. Any one buying a security carrying a fixed income, whether a bond or a preferred or guaranteed stock, must face the probability of a fall in the price of his investment. On the other hand, those who put their money into property or certificates of interest in corporations which give them the right to participate in the profits of industry, can look forward to a steady appreciation in the money value of their investments.

These statements challenge attention. I have stated them in the baldest possible manner, so that the issues which they raise can be set forth with entire distinctness. If the depreciation of gold continues, bonds must come down and stocks must rise. If a survey of the situation shall lead us to the conclusion that the depreciation of gold will at no distant date work its own remedy in arresting the increase in the production of gold, then these pessimistic utterances can be subject to the moderating influence of a heavy discount.

XXIII

PRICE MOVEMENTS SINCE 1865

In the previous chapter we reviewed the pessimistic conclusions expressed by Mr. Theodore H. Price concerning the future of bond prices. These conclusions are, in effect, that the prices of fixed interest bonds will continue to decline, while the prices of commodities and land will continue to advance, and they are based upon the assumption that the supply of gold will continue to increase for an indefinite period.

In order to see what basis there is for this conclusion, it is necessary to examine into the history of gold production and prices. This is not the first experience the world has had with high prices. In fact, the prices of 1911, measured by the quotations of forty years ago, are extremely moderate. The highest prices ever reached since accurate records have been kept were in 1873, when the average of 45 staple articles of commerce stood at 111 per cent. of the average from 1867 to 1877, which was taken as the standard. From this point, during the next twenty years, prices rapidly declined, until in 1896, when the lowest point was reached, they stood at only 61 per cent. of the standard, a decline of 50 points in twenty-three years.

This fall of prices was primarily due to a marked falling-off in the production of gold, which began in 1865, and continued until the lowest point was reached in 1883. While the output of gold mines was declining, industry and trade continued to advance, and the result was a very large increase in the demand for gold falling upon a stationary or declining supply. Prices, therefore, suffered the serious decline already indicated. This fall of prices coincided with a series of disastrous commercial panics, followed by periods of long depression, in which bankruptcies were numerous, the number of unemployed large, prices declining, and trade stagnant and depressed. During this period, the question of the fall of prices agitated the world even more than the difficulties connected with the rise of prices perplex it to-day. Here and there a man of intelligence was found to express the opinion that the fall of prices was a benefit, but the consensus of opinion was that it was an unmitigated evil.

Writing in the *Journal of the Royal Statistical*

THE CAREFUL INVESTOR

Society for September, 1886, Mr. Augustus Sauerbeck, who has long enjoyed the reputation of the
world's greatest price-statistician, summed up the
situation as follows:

A decline of prices, so far as occasioned by a reduction in the
cost of production, is a decided advantage for the consumer, as
his principle will always be, "the cheaper the better." The
lower classes have therefore improved their position, as wages
have only moderately fallen, while they can buy most of their
requirements at lower prices. Altogether, they are much better
off than in the first half of the century, and what was formerly
considered a luxury forms now part of their daily wants.

If we, however, say "the cheaper the better," we must not
forget that "cheap" is a relative expression, and cannot mean
"the lower the better." If all prices, or the prices of most of
the principal articles, fall, then it is a distinct disadvantage to
all producing classes; they either lose heavily or have their
profits curtailed. Capital is reduced, or does not increase at the
usual ratio, and ultimately the loss to the whole community
must be much greater than any small advantage to the consumer.

A real benefit is only derived by the classes with fixed incomes,
and by capitalists possessing consols and similar safe investments,
who can buy more commodities with their income. Many, however, had their interests reduced by one per cent., and their
income, therefore, say, by 20 to 25 per cent. . . .

Producers have been the severest sufferers, and particularly
those of agricultural produce, who had to sustain the strong
competition of cheap soil in extra-European countries, which
became more effective by the reduction of freight and charges.
The consequence was a general decline in the value of land. . . .

The ultimate range of prices is, on the whole, immaterial, as
it is not prices, but quantities, which keep people employed; but
it is not at all immaterial how prices move, and every strong
decline is accompanied by a severe crisis. The income is reduced,

and people find it difficult or impossible to retrench, particularly if luxury has increased during a period of great prosperity. It is the period of transition under which we suffer, and when this is passed we may again expect better times.

The better times which Mr. Sauerbeck predicted did not arrive for ten years after the article from which the above quotation was taken appeared. The depression which he portrayed in such moderate terms continued to spread, with only occasional respites, caused by bountiful crops or some similar temporary relief, until 1896. Contrary to the belief generally held, that the investor profited by this decline of prices and the resulting depression, the reverse was the case. The investor suffered quite as severely as any other class. As prices declined, the profits of industry diminished, and the margin of security which is found, not in the case of productive property, but in its profitableness, rapidly diminished. At intervals, as a result of this decline in profits, came wholesale outbreaks of bankruptcy, in which the soundest and strongest corporations were carried down to ruin, inflicting enormous losses upon investors. Bond-holders and stock-holders alike were involved in this catastrophe. This was the period which saw the bankruptcy of the Union Pacific, the Northern Pacific, the Reading, and the Atchison, Topeka and Santa Fe. Ten years before their failures, which followed the panic of 1893, four of these five railroads were ranked among the strong railroad enterprises of the country. Their failures affected bond-holders and stock-holders alike.

The security of bonds was weakened by the decline of prices, and the investor found slight compensation in the advance of the prices of those of his holdings which survived the shock for the impairment of his security. At the same time, when he came to invest his surplus income in any security, the number of staple investments, owing to the persistence of depression and bankruptcy, was so much reduced as to carry the prices of strong investments to figures at which they yielded between 3 and 3½ per cent, on the purchase price. It is a mistaken notion that the investor profits during periods of falling prices. He suffers in common with the rest of the community. Falling prices, due to a scarcity of gold, are an evil. A downward movement of prices blights enterprises, discourages producers, and injures the investor in hardly less degree.

It is from this industrial slough of despond

that the large increase in gold-production, which began in 1886, and has continued until the last few years, has rescued the civilized world. The past ten years have been years of world-wide and abounding prosperity, in which every class has participated. It is true that real wages—that is, the purchasing power of money wages over the necessaries of life—have declined, but, on the other hand, the aggregate of wages received, owing to the abundant opportunities for employment, has been far greater than it was during the low-priced years which preceded. The producing classes have everywhere prospered. The value of land has greatly advanced, and the farmer in every country in the world has established his financial position on a basis of prosperity.

The investors have also profited. In so far as they held stocks, they have seen these stocks rise to high figures. If they held mortgages, they have had these mortgages promptly paid, in striking contrast to the frequent necessity of foreclosure which characterized the years following the panic of 1893. If the security of their bonds had been impaired by the previous years of depression, the years of prosperity have repaired the damage done, and elevated to the class of sound investments a very large number of railroad and industrial investments, whose previous reputation had been bad. The rise of prices, and the spread and permanence of industrial prosperity, have also brought before the investor large numbers of issues, as, for example, timber bonds and mining bonds, which, during periods of depression, it would not be safe for him to touch. These new securities, together with the large and growing class of public utility bonds, offer him rates of income far greater than those which were open to him in safe investments twenty years ago. If the investor has suffered in the depreciation of high-grade securities in recent years, he has obtained compensation several times over in increased opportunities for investment at higher rates of interest and the increased security of his holdings.

XXIV

INVESTOR AND THE FUTURE OF PRICES

EVERY one who discusses the price question takes it for granted that prices will continue to advance, borne up on a constantly rising money-supply. As the prices of commodities go up, the prices of bonds, and all other forms of fixed interest investment will decline. The purchasing power of salaries, rents, etc., will fall, the assets of large investment institutions will be depleted, and the investing class, generally, will suffer severe losses. On the other hand, it is urged that the advance in prices of commodities will put up the prices of stocks, and all forms of property except loans, rental investments, or annuities. The conclusion drawn from this prediction is that the investor should discriminate against bonds and in favor of stocks and real property.

If, however, it appears upon examination that there is no warrant for believing that the supply of gold will continue to increase as it has in the past; if we reach the conclusion that the gold supply will advance much less rapidly in the next two decades than it has in the past, it is safe to predict that prices will not go much higher.

Before taking up the question of the future supply of gold, let us look for a moment at the other side of the price ratio. A large part of the advance in commodity prices has been due to the pressure of population upon the means of sustenance. In 1890, thirty-six out of every hundred inhabitants of the United States lived in cities and towns of more than 2,500 inhabitants. In 1910, the percentage of city and town dwellers had increased to forty-six. The population of the cities during this twenty-year period rose from 22,700,000 to 46,600,000, while the population of the farms rose from 40,237,000 to 49,348,000. This is a gain of 20,000,000 people for the towns, and 9,000,000 for the farms. In other words, the consumptive demand for food-products is increasing much more rapidly than the number of people available to produce the food.

An examination of the yield of our principal cereal crops confirms this conclusion. In 1889 there was a record corn-crop in the United States, and the total production reached 2.1 billion bushels. By 1911 the production had risen only to 2.5 billion bushels. The yield per acre in 1889 was 27 bushels, and in 1911 about 24 bushels. The wheat-yield of the United States in 1889 was 490,000,000 bushels, and in 1911, 621,000,000 bushels. The yield per acre was almost the same, 12.9 bushels in 1889 and 12.5 bushels in 1911.

The statistics of farm animals make even a more disastrous showing. In 1890 there were 57,648,000 cattle on American farms; in 1911 the number had increased only to 60,502,000, although the total population of the country during the same period had risen from 62,947,000 to 91,972,000. The showing for hogs is but little better: 50,625,000 in 1890, and 65,620,000 in 1911.

These few comparisons prove conclusively that one cause of the advance of prices has been the diminishing yield from the farms, at a time when the demand for food-stuffs was greatly increased by the growth in city population. It is unreasonable to suppose that this condition will be allowed long to continue. Farming is, at the present time, the most profitable American industry, and yet American farms, if cultivated with intelligence and with sufficient capital, could easily double their yield. It is a poor farm that cannot show 50 bushels of corn to the acre, and yet the average for the United States is less than 24 bushels. A yield of 20 bushels of wheat to the acre, with ordinary cultivation and care, is not excessive. The average yield for the United States, however, is only 12. Yields of oats from 50 to 60 bushels to the acre are very commonly secured by intelligent and competent farmers. The average yield for the United States is only 24.4 bushels.

The widespread agitation of this subject of rising prices of farm-lands, and the growing interest of all classes in the problem of food-supply, is certain to result in a very great increase in the production of agricultural products during the next decade, and it is a reasonable presumption that farm products will be lower as a result. While the yield from farms already in cultivation will increase, enormous areas of new land are being opened up. The completion of the Grand Trunk Pacific in Canada is certain to make large additions to the wheat supply. The agricultural area of the Argentine Republic is rapidly expanding, stimulated by the enormous profits to be gained from wheat-growing. Agriculture, the world over, is feeling the stimulus of high prices and immense profits. The natural consequence will be a continued increase in the supply of food-stuffs, and fall in their prices.

INVESTOR AND FUTURE PRICES

Space does not permit a review of the corresponding developments in other lines of raw-material production. It is sufficient to point out that the production of coal, iron, wool, cotton, copper, and, indeed, all of the materials of industry, is advancing rapidly, and that the tendency everywhere seems to be toward lower prices as a result.

What now of the gold supply? Are we warranted in believing that the supply of gold will continue to increase, and that its value will progressively decline? It is impossible, on the basis of an examination of the history of gold-production, to reach such a conclusion. On the contrary, the indications are abundant that gold-production for the next few years has nearly, if not quite, reached its maximum, and that the production will continue to decline.

Gold has a fixed price—$20.67 an ounce. The gold-miner is producing money. Out of his daily production, he must pay his expenses. He buys labor, timber, drill steel, candles, lubricating oil, quicksilver, wood, sulphuric acid, salt, scrap iron, and rope, in addition to large amounts of machinery. He also hires a variety of skilled labor, besides many unskilled workmen. The lower the prices of these materials and the lower the wages of labor, the larger will be the margin which remains out of his daily production of money.

When prices fall, and when labor is cheap and abundant, this margin is large. As a result, the gold-miner makes large profits; investors are anxious to put their money in his business. Prospectors are active in discovering new deposits. The annual production is extended to ores yielding, in some cases, less than $3.00 a ton. A large increase in the output of gold is the result. When prices are rising, however, the margin of the gold-miner's profits is reduced. The rising prices, which increase the profits of other industries, compel him to pay more for his labor. The investor's money is directed into other channels than gold-mining. The prospecting activities, no longer stimulated by lack of opportunity for employment, on the one hand, and by the glittering prizes of discovery on the other, slacken. The gold-miner is forced to abandon the immense bodies of low-yield ore. As a result, gold-production declines.

This movement is at present taking place in every gold-mining country. Those who are counting on an increase in the production of gold should examine the statistics of gold-production in the United States. The principal gold-mining States are Alaska, California, Colorado, Montana, Nevada, South Dakota, and Utah. Of these seven States, only one shows any large increase in gold production, the State of Nevada, due to the development of a few camps of extraordinary richness. The production in Alaska, which was $18,000,000 in 1907, in 1911 was only $16,000,000. Colorado in 1905 produced $25,000,-000 of gold; in 1911 only $19,000,000. The production of Montana, during the same period, fell from $5,000,000 to a little more than $3,000,000. South Dakota about held its own. The production of Utah seriously declined. The production of Nevada, during the same period, rose from $5,000,000 to $19,000,000, and the production for the United States increased from $88,000,000 to $96,000,000, an increase due to the phenomenal discoveries in a single State.

These figures show that the gold-mining industry, taking the Western country as a whole, is declining, the natural inference from the extraordinary prosperity in competing industries throughout this section. Even taking the figures for the entire world, there is no reason to anticipate a continuance of the rate of increase. In 1906 the total production of the world was $402,-000,000. Five years later it was $455,000,000. These annual increases in production, it must be remembered, are added to a stock of gold which has now reached immense proportions, so that the percentage of increase is small. It must also be remembered that the demands for money are rapidly increasing—increasing, indeed, far more rapidly than a gain of ten or fifteen million dollars a year can satisfy. Take, for example, the national banks of the United States, In 1900 these banks held in specie $373,000,000, nearly all of this being gold. In 1911, twelve years later, the specie holdings had increased to $711,-000,000, more than double the former amount.

Every time a new bank is organized, and the number is rapidly increasing, a certain amount of money must be withdrawn from circulation and put into that bank's reserve. This represents an increasing demand upon the world's money supply. What is going on in the United States is but typical of development in other countries. Canada and South America are rapidly enlarging their banking reserves. Immense amounts of gold will be sent to China to assist in the industrial development of that country. The final settlement of the Turkish problem will open the resources of the Balkan Peninsula to exploitation, and large amounts of money will be required to carry on this new business. In every part of the world, in vast regions, until recent years untouched by civilization, railroads are being constructed, mines opened, farms developed, and money—that is, gold—required.

In view of the small increases in the annual production of gold, and in view also of the certainty that the next decade will see large increases in the production of commodities and in the demand for money, it is unreasonable to expect that prices will much longer continue to increase. The investor who has been discouraged by a decline in the prices of his fixed interest securities, and who has been tempted to sell them out at a sacrifice, or to exchange them for bonds of less merit, but higher yield, will do well to remember that economic history always repeats; that there have been periods of rising prices in the past, and that these have always been followed by other periods when prices were declining and bonds increasing in value.

INDEX

INDEX

INDEX

287

INDEX

"Matching" orders, 29
Monopoly of control of raw material, 215
  example, 148, 149
Mortgage bank, advantages, 203
  in Germany, illustration, 202
  in United States, 204
  Lombard Investment Co. failure, 204
  need of, 203
  where found, 203
  work of, 203
Mortgage bondholder, rights of, 59
  nature of lien, 50–52
  given by business corporation, 58
Muck-raking magazines, 11
Municipal Bonds: careful legal investigation (Helena, Mont. example), 104
  history of in U. S., 100
  Lawrence Chamberlain, 107
  lawyer's statement to bond house, 106
  levee district, illustration, 111
  remedy in case of default, 113
  restrictions, 100–102, 110
  safety of, 108
  security of, 99
  special assessment bonds, 113
  tax district, illustration, 111
  yields, prevailing, 109
"Municipal Bonds Held Void," 103
Municipal ownership and operation, 176

National banks of United States, specie holdings, 282
  Canada, 282
  South America, 282
Net income of American people, 36
Newspaper editorials, 12
New York Central & Hudson River Railroad, profits, 138
New York City transit, illustration, 174

New York merchant, illustration, 27
Northern Pacific, bankruptcy, 272
Notes and paper outstanding, industrial corporations, 241

Panic of 1837, 94
Patent monopoly, 213
Peckham, Justice, 148
Pennsylvania Railroad Co., compared with U. S. Steel Corp., 120, 121
  freight classification, 210
  profits, 138
Personal equation, 217
Philadelphia Exchange, commissions 26
Philadelphia Rapid Transit systems, 143, 170–174
Pools, 29, 30
Population, necessity of growth, 156
  increases, 198
Powers of attorney, 41
Powerlessness of small stockholders, 44
Predictions, difficulty of, 29
Price movements: decline, 271, 272
  increases, 262
  rising, of operating supplies, 140
  Sauerbeck, 270
  wholesale, 106
Price, Theodore H., 261–266, 268
Price, Waterhouse & Co., 159
Privileges of stockholders, 41
Professional stock market educators, 28
Profit regulation by state, 150
Profitableness of gambling, 26
Prosperity of past ten years, 150
Prouty, Charles A., 134
Proxies, 41
Public Service Commissions, Act creating Public Service Commission of New York, 178
  attitude of financial interests, 184

288

INDEX

INDEX